W9-DCH-831

Broadcast Voice Handbook

How to Polish Your On-Air Delivery

Second Edition

Ann S. Utterback, Ph.D.

Bonus Books, Inc., Chicago

99   98   97   96   5   4   3   2

Library of Congress Cataloging-in-Publication Data

Utterback, Ann S.
    Broadcast voice handbook : how to polish your on-air delivery / Ann S. Utterback. — 2nd ed.
        p.   cm.
    Includes bibliographical references and index.
    ISBN 1-56625-022-6
    1. Radio announcing.   2. Television announcing.   3. Voice culture.
    4. Broadcasting—Vocational guidance.   I. Title.
    PN1991.8.A6U87   1995
    808.5′1—dc20   95-18254
                                                                      CIP

Bonus Books, Inc.
160 East Illinois Street
Chicago, Illinois 60611

Printed in the United States of America

Voice is probably the #1 criterion used in hiring. When News Directors punch the eject button 15 seconds into an applicant's tape, they do it because that applicant sounds like an amateur, not a professional. . . . If you're going to make your living with your voice, you should learn to use your voice effectively. It is as basic as learning how to type, and for a broadcaster it is just as important.

David Cupp
News Director, WVIR–TV
Charlottesville, Virginia

Even the most brilliantly written and produced news story can be ruined by a poor delivery or an untrained voice. Likewise, a skillful, expressive delivery can liven up a mediocre package and make it seem special.

Pat Dolan
News Director, News 12 Long Island
Woodbury, New York

Courtesy of KSL–TV, Salt Lake City, UT

Courtesy of KGO Radio, San Francisco, CA

The effect of a broadcaster's voice is immediate and overpowering. No amount of excellent writing or good on-air presence can compensate for a poor voice.

Susan L. Stolov
President
Washington Independent Productions
Washington, D.C.

Vocal delivery always has and always will play a major part in broadcast news. And while content is how a good piece should be judged, the audience has to hear the story first. If they don't like how you sound, they'll miss the rest.

Bob Bartlett
News Director, KTAB–TV
Abilene, Texas

Contents

Quick Reference to Common Broadcast Voice Problems

Acknowledgments

A project like this is always based on the support of many people. My thanks date back over twenty years to my colleagues at Memphis State University. I thank Mike Osborn for shoving a voice and diction book in my hand and telling me I was going to begin teaching voice and diction, and Jack Sloan for providing the continued opportunity to teach at Memphis State. David Yellin taught me to respect the television medium and the people who work in it. Working with Yellin's friends, such as Fred Freed and Paul Bogart, was invaluable to my development. I am grateful to Betty May Collins Parker and Lea Queener for sharing their extensive knowledge and inspiring me with their continuing interest in the field of voice improvement.

I was fortunate to have the opportunity to attend Isaac Brackett's classes during my doctoral work at Southern Illinois University. As an outstanding speech pathologist, Dr. Brackett's help was immeasurable.

News directors across the country have contributed to this project. You will see many of their names throughout the book and in Appendix B. I would especially like to thank Jim Rutledge, former Assistant Bureau Chief of the CNN Washington Bureau, who first suggested I concentrate my professional interests in broadcast voice. Mike Freedman has been supportive of my work for a number of years, and I am honored to include his foreword in this book. I would also like to thank Sue Stolov, president of Washington Independent Productions, for her careful reading of the manuscript and for giving me confidence in my work from the very beginning. Other news directors, including Dave Cupp, Dan Shelley, Brian Olson, John Macdonald, and Bob Priddy, have also been supportive since the beginning, and I thank them.

I am grateful to Lillian Rae Dunlap and the University of Missouri-Columbia for administering the news director survey and compiling the statistics presented in Appendix A. Warm thanks go to Faith Duvall-Menestrina for her help with the statistics and for her friendship.

I want to thank my clients, who are often my most important teachers. They have all taught me about the realities of working in broadcast news, and I honor them for sharing their feelings with me. I am especially grateful to the broadcasters at the Voice of America who come to me from forty-seven different language services. They have taught me not just about voice but about the world as well.

I am grateful to the people at Bonus Books, and I am indebted to the Radio-Television News Directors Association for their continuing support of my work.

I dedicate this book to my husband and closest friend, Jim, whose constant love and encouragement have shown me, "It can be."

Special thanks to J. and M.
who helped me find my voices

Ann S. Utterback, Ph.D.

Foreword to the Second Edition

The voice is to the broadcaster as the hands are to the pianist. Just as a musical score is enhanced by the expertise and enthusiasm of the artist, the written word is transformed into meaningful information for the ear by the eloquence and style of the broadcaster.

An effective broadcast voice requires training, practice and care. The finest in the profession understand their role as communicators and the importance of the voice in the process. While they do not sound alike, they share important common traits. They are articulate, authoritative and conversational. They understand the difference between simply reading copy and conveying information in a manner that draws the listener or viewer to the broadcast. It is an art. As such, the voice becomes the brush that paints pictures for the mind's eye.

Listen to the classic broadcasts of Edward R. Murrow from London or Walter Cronkite following the death of President John F. Kennedy. These are classic examples of important information being delivered by consummate professionals. These riveting broadcasts stir emotions, yet maintain a sense of calm through calamity.

Aspiring broadcasters are advised to articulate, enunciate, breathe from the diaphragm, sound authoritative, stay calm under fire and, all the while, be conversational! This must seem an impossible combination at first. Yet, through training, practice and care, the voice becomes polished and the procedures routine. Notice it is usually the novice who sounds quite different on the air than off.

Professionals sound the same in normal conversation as they do when the microphone is on.

Over the course of my twenty-five-year association with broadcast journalism, it has been encouraging to see a renewed enthusiasm for training and care of the voice. Seminars on the subject at Radio-Television News Directors Association conferences draw standing-room-only audiences. These sessions are consistently among the highest rated at RTNDA functions. They are moderated by Ann Utterback.

I have also seen the results of Ann's work first-hand. As vice president and managing editor for the broadcast division of United Press International, I invited Ann to work with staff members of our radio network. The improvement among those who studied with her was remarkable. They not only sounded better on the air, they felt better about themselves. They learned that all voices are special and distinctive, and often, minor modification and practice can transform an adequate voice into an excellent one.

It is indeed an honor to contribute to this excellent handbook. With it, Ann Utterback is helping to rekindle a vital light in the industry: the delivery of the message and the importance of "The Broadcast Voice."

Michael Freedman
Director, Public Affairs
The George Washington University

President
Washington, D.C., Chapter
Radio-Television News Directors Association

Voice training is vital to broadcast communication, and yet it's one of the last things many TV reporters/anchors are concerned with. Proper breathing technique, articulation, and interpretation of copy can help set people apart from the pack when competing for jobs.

Mike Rindo
News Director, WWMT–TV
Kalamazoo, Michigan

Bad delivery is the biggest reason I find not to hire an applicant. The voice communicates so much, yet there's an overemphasis on appearance. I find a lot more voice problems than appearance problems.

Dave Busiek
News Director, KCCI–TV
Des Moines, Iowa

It's not hard to find people with good qualifications in broadcasting, even among the entry-level candidates. But their vocal quality is often *one of the key factors I use to weed out the real contenders from the "also rans."*

Doug Maughan
News Director, KMVT–TV
Twin Falls, Idaho

Introduction to the Second Edition

As the second edition of *Broadcast Voice Handbook* goes to press, we are beginning a trip onto the information superhighway. Experts are debating exactly what broadcast journalism will consist of in the twenty-first century. But two things are certain: vocal delivery will remain important and "live" work will be on the increase. As technology changes at a rapid rate, it is comforting to know that the vocal mechanism we use has been around for at least a half million years. Learning how your voice works and how you can improve and care for it will give you information that will last a lifetime.

This second edition of *Broadcast Voice Handbook* offers me an opportunity to share my professional growth of the last five years. My work with broadcasters has expanded, and it is rewarding to be able to expand my book as well. You will find two new chapters in this edition. Chapter 6, "Sounding Conversational," offers an interpersonal communication approach to broadcast delivery. This approach can be coupled with the marking process presented in Chapter 5 or used as a separate approach to a conversational delivery.

Chapter 7, "Coping With Stress," is most indicative of my professional growth since I wrote the first edition of *Broadcast Voice Handbook.* I once felt that to improve your voice you could concentrate on the vocal mechanism. Fix the problems there, and you fix the voice. I now take a much more complete approach to voice. I have found that I can teach clients everything I know about the mechanics of voice, but they will not improve if their body or mind is physically or emotionally stressed. We speak with our whole bodies, and effective broadcast voice work must be holistic in its approach. Chapter 7 gives ways to deal with the stress of working in the news business and methods for keeping your workplace healthy.

When the first edition of *Broadcast Voice Handbook* came out in 1990, I had been working almost exclusively with broadcasters since 1985. Before that I had spent sixteen years teaching college students, corporate executives, and government officials how to use their voices well. I wrote in the introduction to the first edition that when I began working with broadcasters I assumed because they make their livings with their voices, they are trained to use their voices more effectively than most professionals.

After working more than ten years with hundreds of radio and television broadcasters in this country and in Canada, I am sad to report this is not the case. I continue to see increasing numbers of clients who do not know how to breathe correctly or use their voices to enhance the meaning of their copy. These clients range from recent college graduates to broadcast veterans with thirty years of experience who have risen to the network level. Most have a basic lack of knowledge about how to care for their voices and use them effectively.

What broadcasters do have is a real desire to learn more about voice. I realized this when I was asked to lecture at the 1988 Radio-Television News Directors Association conference in Las Vegas. I was told to expect around thirty participants. When three hundred participants showed up for that lecture, I saw that knowledge about how to use your voice effectively was an area of great interest in the broadcasting community throughout the country. The top rating that lecture received reinforced this conclusion. I continue to lecture at the RTNDA International Conferences in this country and in Canada, and the positive responses to my lectures illustrate that voice is of paramount importance to news directors and broadcasters. News directors make comments to me like, "It's great to be a good journalist, but if the voice is bad the audience won't want to listen." Reading over the news directors' comments in Appendix B, you will hear this sentiment repeated.

In addition to the need for voice work for professionals who are on the air, I have learned that there is much frustration among news directors about the lack of voice training that broadcast journalism students get while in college. As one Baltimore, Maryland, news director puts it: "The proper use of the voice is paramount and is probably one of the most overlooked areas in college training." Many of my clients have voiced this same frustration. I remember one young woman telling me her father was not pleased that he had to pay a consultant to work with her during her last semester of college when he was already paying tuition. Unfortunately, her university did not offer any assistance with voice improvement. Steven Smith, News Director at WWTV in Cadillac, Michigan, sees the same problem:

> Voice and delivery are the two biggest problems
> I encounter on resume tapes. Colleges and universities pay little, if any, attention to this concern. Ninety percent of the tapes I review are
> rejected based on poor voice and/or delivery.

This book provides the information that is needed in the newsroom and the classroom to help broadcasters develop and maintain healthy voices that enhance meaning. You will not find a quick technique in this book that will give you an instant broadcast voice. Breaking old habits and developing new ones takes time. In order to have a better broadcast voice, you must learn how your vocal mechanism works and practice the exercises that will allow new habits to be formed.

The days of training everyone to sound the same are gone. Luckily, in this country we no longer have a set broadcast model. I call that old announcer's voice the "Ted Baxter" delivery from the character on *The Mary Tyler Moore Show.* That voice is now being revived by the "Jim Dial" character on the *Murphy Brown* television show. Both of these characters mimic the staid, low-pitched delivery that was once a standard in broadcasting.

There is much more acceptance of different types of voices in broadcasting now than there was twenty years ago, but this acceptance does not mean that voice is not important. I hear this warning from more and more news directors. They feel that just because we are not teaching all newscasters to sound like Edward R. Murrow, this does not negate the need for training.

In order to get the most out of any voice, you must know the basic anatomy of speech and the fundamentals of how you can use your voice effectively. Basic knowledge about breathing, producing sound, resonating sound, and shaping sound into words is essential for good vocal production. Broadcasters cannot begin to develop a method of stressing words, for example, without knowing how breathing relates to stressing.

In addition to the challenge of knowing the anatomy of speech in order to maintain a healthy voice, broadcasters need to develop a relaxed, conversational delivery. Establishing this natural, conversational delivery is not something that most people can accomplish without a systematic approach. Such a delivery involves breath control, pacing, and stress and intonation. Broadcasters must learn how to sound as if they are talking with someone when they are actually reading. And, as a California news director points out, this situation is as important in television as in radio: "Ninety-five percent of TV news reporting is voice-over. . . . Competent and compelling storytellers are the people we look for, people who can not only write to video but can hold the audience with the power of their voice."

The old notion that broadcasters are "announcers" is gone. Comfortable "communicators" are what the public wants. The challenge to broadcasters is to be able to relax enough in a tense situation to maintain a healthy voice and sound relaxed. In addition, listeners want them to pull out the meaning of the story with their voices. This is a difficult challenge.

This book provides the information needed to meet this challenge. *Broadcast Voice Handbook* is as simple and straightforward as possible. The contents are organized in a sequential manner. It begins with the production of the breath, which is the energy for speech and moves through the production and resonating of sound waves to the articulation of the sound and finally the methods of stressing for meaning and sounding conversational.

The International Phonetic Alphabet is used as a method of presenting the sounds of our language. All phonetic symbols in the book appear in slash marks (e.g., /k/).

It is recommended that you read the chapters in the order presented so that you will understand how the processes are interrelated. Even if you read the material quickly without completely retaining it, you will get an important basic understanding of vocal production.

In addition to gaining a basic understanding of vocal production, it is also necessary to develop a respect for your voice. After all, if you are a broadcaster you are making your living on two tiny pieces of muscle in your throat. Broadcasters need to recognize the importance of a healthy voice. Think of your voice as an instrument. Not many concert pianists would abuse their fingers or ballet dancers their legs, but many broadcasters abuse their voices daily.

If you ask even a young ballerina about the hamstring or the Achilles tendon, she can usually tell you where it is and its function. I do not find this basic knowledge of vocal anatomy with many of my clients. Most are amazed when they see photographs of the vocal folds and realize how delicate the tissue is. These same newscasters would want to fire a cameraperson who did not know the basic mechanics of how television equipment works. They expect a cameraperson to have respect and knowledge of television equipment while they lack the same respect and knowledge of their own vocal equipment.

Knowing the fundamentals of vocal production is only the beginning of the process of voice improvement. Just as a pianist or a dancer must practice daily to maintain their skill, broadcasters must learn that voice improvement is a lifetime pursuit. Maintaining a good broadcast voice takes hours of practice and a lifetime of respect.

The Warm-Ups at the end of each chapter can become part of your daily routine. These sections have been marked with arrows for your easy reference. Each Warm-Up section is preceded by some exercises that help you become familiar with the chapter concepts. These are called "Focus on Breathing," "Focus on Phonation," etc.

Once you are familiar with the concept, you might want to put your favorite Warm-Ups on index cards or a sheet of paper to post over your desk or in the sound booth to help you remember to practice them. Many of my clients find they like to do Warm-Ups while driving. It is especially helpful to do articulation Warm-Ups in the morning while driving to work. This is usually one time for practice that works with even the busiest schedule. You should find other times as well because continued practice is of utmost importance in changing or maintaining vocal habits.

This book can serve as a lifetime reference companion as you continue to respect your voice by monitoring your vocal production throughout your career. It gives you the basic knowledge you need to maintain a healthy, effective voice.

One of the ironies of a good broadcast voice is that the better it is, the less it is noticed. Andy Cassells, Bureau Chief of Cox Broadcasting in Washington, D.C., feels strongly about this: "Voice in a news story should not be noticed. If it is, something is wrong!"

Bill Headline, Vice President and Bureau Chief of CNN's Washington bureau explains, "A broadcast voice should be trained, controlled, and modulated to the point that you are aware not of the voice but of the information that it is delivering."

News directors think of voice as a primary factor in hiring. David Cupp, News Director of WVIR–TV in Charlottesville, Virginia, explains his approach:

> Vocal concerns are so important to me that when I'm hiring the first thing I do is literally turn my back on each applicant's tape. I don't want the distraction of pictures. I don't even want to know what an applicant looks like until I have had a chance to listen carefully.

A broadcaster's voice should be a medium that delivers information to the listener. It should never get in the way of this information. Only a healthy voice that is controlled by a broadcaster can be effective in this task. Through continued awareness of your broadcast voice and exercise to keep it healthy and effective, you can make your vocal instrument work for you.

Courtesy of the Voice of America, Washington, D.C.

Building a good voice is like building a house. They both must have a good foundation to be strong. Learning correct diaphragmatic breathing is the foundation. Breath control techniques are as essential for an announcer as they are for an opera singer. The singer must control a note for effect—an announcer must control to complete a message. Without proper breathing techniques as a base for delivery, there is no way an announcer can get his or her message across.

Robert L. Runda
Chief, Broadcast Announcing Division
Trainer, Military Broadcasters
Indianapolis, Indiana

Don't overlook the importance of pauses in an audio passage—conversation is filled with pauses, breathing space.

Mick Jensen
News Director, KVOA–TV
Tucson, Arizona

Breathing— The Key to Good Vocal Production

"Try to relax." That is the advice I give clients every day. But the truth is, if you are a journalist working in broadcasting in the 1990s, it is difficult advice to follow. Radio and television news professionals work in a world of live reports, crises, and deadlines. The pressures and tension in television and radio broadcasting are enormous, and, for the most part, they are unavoidable. Many of you may feel the phrase "relaxed broadcaster" is an oxymoron.

A television reporter, for example, works on a schedule that demands tension and pressure. To meet a 5:00 p.m. news show deadline, a typical reporter has from 9:00 a.m. to around 4:30 p.m. to produce one or more packages. Most of the day the reporter runs all over the city interviewing people to develop a story. As the deadline approaches, the reporter must shoot a stand-up looking and sounding composed and in control. Voice-overs must be recorded in the sound booth as the deadline gets ever closer. The tension that has helped this reporter succeed in the fact-gathering part of the day now becomes a handicap (see Chapter 7).

This hectic schedule is accepted practice for broadcasters. Few other occupations demand this level of output. Most business

A typical Washington television news bureau reporter might end
the day viewing one of as many as three packages she did that day.

Courtesy of Washington Independent News, Washington, D.C.

executives have weeks between deadlines. Writers, actors, and other
artists have months before they have to present their creative product. But broadcasters work with daily deadlines week after week.

For a broadcaster's voice to work effectively, relaxation is
the key. Because your voice depends on various muscles in your
body, it reflects the degree of tension you are feeling. Stress affects
all your muscle tone, which affects posture, respiration, and voice
control. A tense body usually means a tense voice.

Proper breathing can be very effective in relieving tension
and improving the voice. Stress control workshops teach diaphragmatic breathing for relaxation. Natural childbirth depends on breathing to help alleviate pain. Concentrating on a long, slow inhalation/
exhalation is often recommended by doctors to control the tension
that exacerbates any type of pain. A long inhalation/exhalation is
also helpful in tense social situations such as a job interview, an
especially rough airline flight, or before giving a speech.

Yoga and other Eastern philosophies have used breathing as part of meditation for centuries. The philosophy of yoga holds as a belief that if you can control the breath, or prana, you can control the mind. This idea can be adapted for broadcasters: If you can control the breath, you can control the voice.

Once you have learned proper abdominal-diaphragmatic breathing as described in the Focus on Breathing section, you can rely on this process to relax you. Your breath is your best ally as a broadcaster. It revitalizes the body while calming the emotions and bringing clarity to the mind. Proper breathing can help break the tension that builds for many broadcasters as their workdays progress.

Proper breathing not only relaxes you, it provides the basic energy for speech. Breathing for life and breathing for speech, however, are not identical processes. Therefore, before you can begin to think of how to improve your broadcast voice by working on stress and intonation, rate, or pitch, you must first focus on the basic function of breathing.

Anchoring the afternoon drive shift at an all-news radio station involves the pressure of coordinating live reports, late-breaking stories, and deadlines by the minute.

Courtesy of WWJ Radio, Detroit, MI

Breathing Anatomy

In order to learn to use your breath properly as a broadcaster, you need to have an understanding of how we breathe. It is not necessary to learn all the muscles and nerves related to the respiratory system, but some basic anatomy will help you improve your breathing.

The Lungs

Most of us assume that we breathe with our lungs. Taking a deep breath is referred to as "filling up the lungs with air." What we may not know is that the lungs are not doing the work of inhalation or exhalation. We depend on various muscles in the chest and abdominal area to keep air circulating into our bodies.

The lungs are important for the transfer of oxygen and carbon dioxide to keep us alive, but without the muscles that control them they could not function. The lungs are like two large sponges in our chest. They are light and porous and would float in water much like a natural bath sponge. The lungs fill the area of the chest, or thoracic cavity, with the heart nestled between them.

Leading into each lung is a tube called a bronchus which, like a tree trunk, spreads roots, called bronchial tubes, into each lung (see Figure 1). These bronchial tubes branch into smaller and smaller tubes, bronchioles, and end as tiny air sacs. These air sacs have capillaries very close to the surface, and this is where the exchange of oxygen and carbon dioxide takes place. This exchange of gases is so fundamental in keeping us alive, that it begins as a reflex action as soon as we take our first breath at birth.

Our first breath is usually accompanied by a loud cry, which indicates the close connection between breathing and speech. To produce that cry, the air exhaled from the lungs goes up the bronchial tubes into the trachea and passes through the larynx which contains the vocal folds (vocal cords) which create sound waves (see Figure 1). That air must be pushed from the lungs, however, since the lungs have no muscles themselves. This is where your understanding of the anatomy of breathing can help you as a broadcaster.

Figure 1
Anatomy Drawing of the Organs Involved in Speech

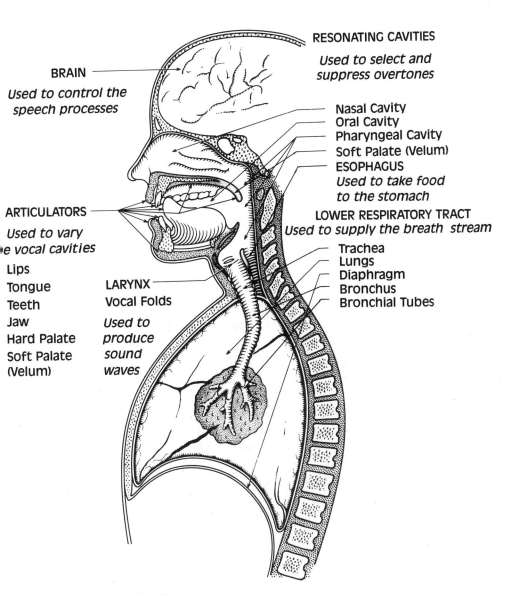

BRAIN

Used to control the speech processes

RESONATING CAVITIES

Used to select and suppress overtones

Nasal Cavity
Oral Cavity
Pharyngeal Cavity
Soft Palate (Velum)
ESOPHAGUS
Used to take food to the stomach

LOWER RESPIRATORY TRACT
Used to supply the breath stream

Trachea
Lungs
Diaphragm
Bronchus
Bronchial Tubes

ARTICULATORS

Used to vary e vocal cavities

Lips
Tongue
Teeth
Jaw
Hard Palate
Soft Palate
(Velum)

LARYNX
Vocal Folds

Used to produce sound waves

Courtesy of AT & T Archives

The Diaphragm

The most important muscle for speech is the diaphragm. The diaphragm muscle is a large sheet-like muscle that separates the thoracic cavity from the abdominal cavity (see Figure 2). The diaphragm bisects the body horizontally starting at the breastbone. It continues along the bottom of the rib cage around to the spine. The diaphragm forms a complete floor for the thoracic cavity. The broad bases of our cone-shaped lungs rest on the diaphragm. This solid muscle is pierced by three important tubes: the esophagus, which takes food to the stomach directly under the diaphragm; the aorta, which takes blood down from the heart; and the vena cava, which brings blood up from the lower part of the body to the heart (see Figure 2).

The action of the diaphragm is what allows us to breathe naturally. In its resting state, the diaphragm muscle is dome-shaped,

Figure 2
The Thorax and Diaphragm (cut-away front view)

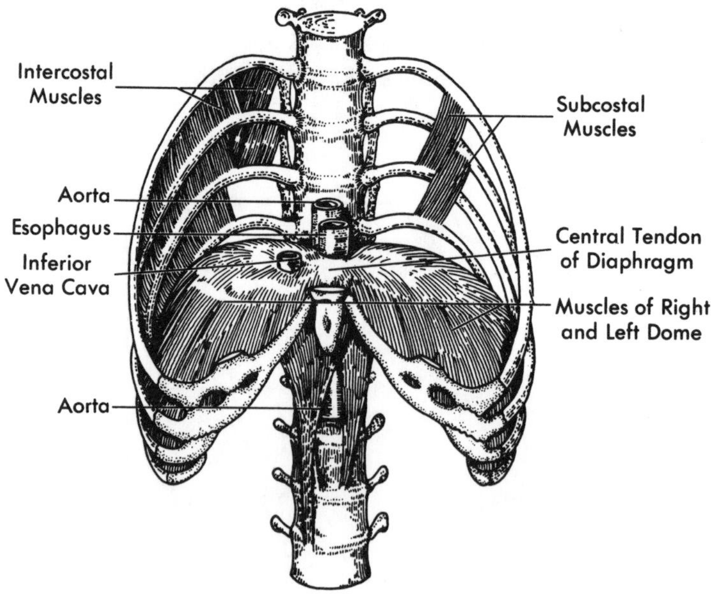

From *Training the Speaking Voice*, Third Edition, by Virgil A. Anderson. Copyright © 1977 by Oxford University Press, Inc. Reprinted by permission.

rising up into the thoracic cavity. When we inhale with the diaphragm, this large, sheet-like muscle contracts and flattens out. As it flattens, it moves downward. The ribs flex upward at the same time. The effect of this is to increase the size of the thoracic cavity (see Figure 3). When this happens, a negative air space is created which results in a partial vacuum. Because the air pressure of our atmosphere is greater outside the body at this point, air rushes into the lungs to equalize the pressure.

As the diaphragm muscle flattens out, it also forces the abdominal area to protrude because of the pressure on the stomach, liver, spleen, and other organs beneath it. This movement of the abdominal area makes diaphragmatic breathing easy to monitor (see Focus on Breathing). With a good abdominal-diaphragmatic breath, you feel expansion in the stomach area as well as all around the back. The lower chest area may expand as much as two and a half inches.

Once the thoracic cavity is enlarged and air has rushed into the lungs, the diaphragm and abdominal muscles work to push the air out with a controlled exhalation. Imagine a bellows filling with

Figure 3
Increase of Volume of Thorax with Inhalation

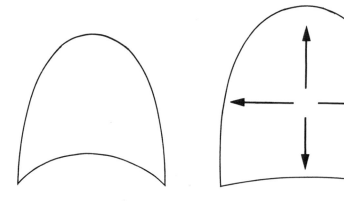

Rib cage before inhalation   Rib cage after inhalation

air. The first step is to enlarge the cavity of the bellows by separating the handles. When the bellows is filled with air, our arm muscles physically control the force of the air as it is blown out. Our abdominal muscles work much the same way by allowing the diaphragm to slowly rise back into its dome-shaped position and the rib cage to return to its original position. This movement forces air out of the lungs with control. For relaxed breathing without the demand of speech, exhalation is simply a relaxation without the control of the abdominal and diaphragm muscles. The elasticity of the rib cage and lungs contributes to the deflation of the lungs in relaxed breathing.

Respiration is a continuous process that keeps us alive. Our body cannot store oxygen. There is a constant demand for it. When our brain feels the oxygen level has dropped, a signal comes from the brain stem to replenish it. This process is so important for life, we cannot voluntarily stop it. Many children's temper tantrums have ended with the threat, "I'll hold my breath until I turn blue." A child may think this is possible, but the involuntary breathing mechanism will take over to keep the child alive.

We breathe from 15,000 to 20,000 times per day. Our lungs normally contain about three quarts of air. We generally inhale and exhale one-half quart of air in quiet respiration when we are breathing twelve to sixteen times per minute. The lungs never completely empty of air. They maintain a residual supply.

The Importance of Abdominal-Diaphragmatic Breathing

Now that you know the anatomy of breathing, you may be wondering why it is important to you as a broadcaster. If the system described above operated naturally, it would not be important. You would go through life, breathing with the diaphragm aided by the abdominal muscles, and your voice would enjoy all the benefits of this type of breathing. Unfortunately, this is not the case.

At some point in our lives we abandon this comfortable breathing for what could be called **socialized breathing.** Someone gives us the message that we should hold in our stomachs and stick out our chests. We could blame physical education teachers or army sergeants for this change, but whether we are male or female, a flat stomach and a large chest become our goals.

Knowing the basics of breathing, you can imagine the results of holding in your stomach and expanding your chest. This forces a type of breathing called upper chest, or clavicular, breathing. The muscles of the chest, or even the higher muscles in the clavicle or collarbone area and the neck muscles do the work of lifting the rib cage to expand it for breathing. Instead of using one of the largest muscles in the body, the diaphragm, which is constructed for the purpose of expanding the rib cage for breathing, we use smaller, less efficient muscles.

When I lecture to convention groups, I often ask the audience to take a deep breath. It is interesting to watch hundreds of people's shoulders heave up and down as they take what they perceive to be a deep breath. Usually only the singers or people who have played a wind instrument know that when taking a deep breath the shoulders do not move. All of the movement is in the abdominal area below the breast bone.

The fear of developing a big stomach area should not keep you from breathing properly. Ironically, abdominal-diaphragmatic breathing may result in a flatter stomach, because it calls for control of the abdominal muscles. They get a better workout when they are used for breathing than when they serve only as a girdle, constantly holding in the stomach area.

Breath Support

As a broadcaster, abdominal-diaphragmatic breathing is one of the best ways to maintain a healthy voice. If the diaphragm and abdominal muscles are doing the work during inhalation and exhalation, the tension involved in breathing is positioned far from the delicate structures in the throat which produce sound waves (laryngeal area). The movement involves the abdominal area moving out and in (see Focus on Breathing). Clavicular breathing, on the other hand, causes the shoulders to rise during inhalation, and increases muscular tension in the neck which may affect the laryngeal area.

(Chapter 2 explains the importance of keeping tension away from the larynx and vocal folds.) In addition, clavicular breathing is shallow breathing, which can be exhausting.

The diaphragm and abdominal muscles give us both the ability to take in a large volume of air and to control exhalation. This is called **breath support**. The amount of time involved in a typical inhalation/exhalation at rest is quite different from the requirements for speech. Our ratio of inhalation to exhalation at rest is close to 1:1. We breathe in for about the same duration as we breathe out. For speech, this ratio must change to 1:5, 1:10, or even greater. In other words, exhalation time is greatly prolonged. We can control the air as it is exhaled if we let the diaphragm and the abdominal muscles do the work. Without control of exhalation, after a deep inhalation air would rush from our lungs as it does when we sigh. This is not conducive to good speech because we cannot say many words during the time it takes to sigh. The air rushes out too rapidly.

Think of a sculptor working on a new creation. Given a small amount of clay, the sculptor's choices are limited. Any sculpture created has to conform to the size of the clay. If the sculptor has a large chunk of clay, the choices are greater. All or part of the clay can be used, and the creation can be large or small depending on the sculptor's concept.

Your breath works in much the same way. When reading broadcast copy you need to have a good supply of air, and you need to be able to control that air. A good air supply gives you the raw material to produce good speech. Proper control of that air will help you mold speech into words that are interesting to hear, easily understood, and full of vocal energy.

Returning to the Natural

You may think at this point that learning to breathe with the diaphragm aided by the abdominal muscles will take months or years of training because it seems so unnatural. Actually, you breathe this way every night when you are sleeping. Have you ever watched a little baby on its back in a crib? The baby's stomach goes up and down, up and down, with each inhalation and exhalation. There is no socialized breathing here. You breathe the same way when you are sleeping, sick, or in a relaxed state, unaware of your breathing. Since none of these apply when you are broadcasting, there is some relearning that must take place, but it need not take long.

A few simple exercises will help you get back in touch with this normal, natural way to breathe. Begin first with the section in this chapter called Focus on Breathing to position your breathing properly. Once you have the correct feeling, proceed to the Breathing Warm-Ups. These should become part of your daily routine to help fight the desire to return to the socialized breathing style.

You should continue practice of abdominal-diaphragmatic breathing in order to increase your breath support. Like any muscle, the diaphragm contracts and relaxes. And like any muscle it can be strengthened through proper exercising. In the same way that pumping iron builds your arm muscles, breathing exercises build your diaphragm and abdominal muscles.

Part of an opera singer's lifetime training is breathing exercises. A singer will spend time lying on the floor with weight on the abdominal area trying to push the weight up. Voice coaches might even put their foot on top of the weight to increase the pressure. All of this is intended to increase the control of the diaphragm and abdominal muscles. When you hear an opera singer hold a note for longer than seems humanly possible, you can bet that singer has worked many hours building breath support. You are listening to the results.

Vocal Benefits of Proper Breathing

What advantages does good breath support have for you as a broadcaster? You certainly do not need to sustain one sound for as long as Luciano Pavarotti or Placido Domingo. What you do need is enough air to be in control of what you are saying. You want to be in control of how long your sentences are and what you can do with your voice. Control of exhalation allows you to vary your delivery rate and duration of sounds. You will also be able to use pitch changes to enhance the meaning of your copy (see Chapter 5).

Poor breathing may result in choppy, disjointed speech. We have all heard broadcasters who have to take a breath pause at the wrong time. The meaning is often changed by an inappropriate pause. The effect is like the old example of "What's that in the road—a head?" In addition, you do not want your limited breath supply to determine how you write. I have had more than one client say to me that they write in short phrases because they run out of air. They do not want to run the risk of an inappropriate pause.

Broadcasters with poor breath support suffer from a number of vocal problems as well. One of the most common is a **glottal fry**. This strange name refers to a popping sound heard toward the ends of sentences when breath supply and pitch drop. The glottis is the opening between the vocal folds, which is where this sound originates. This condition may have gotten its name because the popping sounds like bacon frying. A glottal fry at the ends of sentences usually indicates that breath supply is low, and pitch is near the bottom of the range. Some speakers like Charles Kuralt and Henry Kissinger have glottal fry elements throughout their speech. Normally, however, the glottal fry will begin a few words before the end of a sentence. Increased air supply and a slight rise in pitch will eliminate a glottal fry as long as it is a functional problem and not organic (see Chapter 2).

Another problem that is common with improper breathing is a very high-pitched voice. When we get nervous or anxious, our pitch generally rises because of increased tension in the throat area. Think of a broadcaster at a noisy political convention or covering a rally. In order to be heard over the crowd, the reporter may talk louder and increase the tension in the throat. What we hear is a higher-pitched voice.

One of my clients who was reporting from the Preakness horse race found she had this problem. When she got in the sound booth to do the narration for the package, she realized she had been shouting over exuberant spectators at the race track. Her pitch in her stand-up had been so high she could not match it in the booth. When the package aired, it sounded like two different reporters because of the differing degrees of vocal tension. With proper breathing, she has now learned how to increase her volume without tensing the laryngeal area.

Tension in the laryngeal area also results from upper chest breathing. The tension it takes to increase the size of the chest cavity using the upper chest muscles can move into the laryngeal area. Chapter 2 describes the way the vocal folds work to vary pitch.

Basically, tension causes the folds to become thinner, which produces a higher pitch. If you are breathing in your upper chest, you are increasing the likelihood that your pitch is higher than it should be.

Upper chest breathing may also give you an audible intake of breath. Listeners often complain that they are distracted by the gulps of air they hear reporters taking. That whoosh of air rushing through the mouth can become so predictable it gets in the way of the meaning of the copy.

Taking a good abdominal-diaphragmatic breath before your countdown and another just before you begin your copy will build your air supply (see Breathing Warm-Up 6). This will allow you to take smaller breaths within the copy. It is not possible to take an abdominal-diaphragmatic breath at every pause in your copy. That would be too time-consuming. You have to take short breaths through your mouth when you need air within your copy. When you go to tape for a sound bite or actuality, you may be able to take in another abdominal-diaphragmatic breath. Use every opportunity you have to let the abdominal muscles and the diaphragm do the work.

The Value of Standing for Speech

You will find when doing the Breathing Warm-Ups that standing offers the best posture to fully expand the chest and back area when inhaling. When seated, the abdominal area is pushing up into the dome of the diaphragm. When you stand, the abdominal area is free to expand all around your body. Good singers know this. You rarely see opera singers sing seated. They know that the diaphragm needs freedom to move, and standing allows this.

Most radio studios can accommodate a broadcaster who wants to stand, but many television sound booths are not set up for it. An adjustable mike stand is a small expense, however, when you consider the advantages of standing. CBS once designed a standing desk for Dan Rather, and several other anchors stand even though their desks make them appear seated. They have discovered the advantages of standing.

Some broadcasters have found ingenious ways to free-up the diaphragm. One television network sports announcer who is a

A reporter stands as she voices a story.

Courtesy of KGWN–TV, Cheyenne, WY

former basketball player reportedly kneels in front of the desk in the sound booth. He is well over six feet tall, and kneeling puts him right at mike level. More importantly, it frees the diaphragm by allowing the abdominal area to expand unrestricted.

Another consideration is to avoid the restriction of tight clothing that might keep the abdominal area from expanding. Many broadcasters loosen belts or unbutton waistbands to facilitate easy

A reporter demonstrates a sound booth that could be easily adjusted for standing.

Courtesy of WVIR–TV, Charlottesville, VA

breathing. Ed Bliss, a former CBS writer, reports that Allan Jackson, who reported for CBS Radio for over twenty years, always unbuckled his belt and loosened his pants after he sat down for a broadcast. You may find you need to do this, especially if you have just eaten a large meal. Because the stomach is right below the diaphragm, it is difficult to take a deep breath with a full stomach.

Increasing Vocal Energy

A common problem I see with clients is a lack of vocal energy. Some clients sound like they are bored with what they are reporting. They tell me they do not feel that way, but their voice betrays them.

This is another problem that can be traced to poor air supply. If you feel bad for some reason, it will most likely be heard in your voice. Our voices often reveal our psychological and physiological states. We have all said to someone, "You don't sound like yourself," or "You sound down." Our voices can signal how we feel, and as a broadcaster you must monitor this.

As a listener or viewer, audience members expect broadcasters to be one step above them in energy level. They want to be convinced that the story they are listening to is important enough to take them away from their everyday lives and into the story. If they are driving, your delivery must be more interesting than the passing scenery. If they are at home or at work, you are competing with an infinite number of distractions. You need to pull your listeners up to your energy level to get them to listen. I often notice that within a news story the people being interviewed sound like they have more energy and involvement than the reporter. This indicates low vocal energy and affects the impact of the story.

Oxygen energizes the mind and body. A good inhalation will not only give you the air you need to speak well, it will also give you the vocal energy you need. You will benefit more from three or four deep abdominal-diaphragmatic breaths than you will from three or four cups of coffee. Yogis have used pranayama, the science of breath control, for centuries to achieve a natural high. Proper breathing can help you achieve the vocal energy needed to pull your listener into your story.

Focus on Breathing

Here is a summary of proper inhalation/exhalation for speech:

Inhalation
1. Diaphragm muscle contracts and flattens downward.
2. Ribs flex upward enlarging the chest cavity.
3. Abdominal area protrudes as diaphragm presses on stomach, liver, and other internal organs.

Exhalation
1. Diaphragm begins to relax.
2. Abdominal muscles control relaxation of diaphragm to create breath support.
3. Ribs slowly move down to relaxed position, and
   abdominal area returns to normal position.

Before you can begin doing Warm-Ups for Breathing, you must become familiar with the feeling of abdominal-diaphragmatic breathing. The processes described below will help you focus on the muscles involved.

A) Watch a videotape of yourself taking a deep breath. If you are a television broadcaster watch one of your tapes. Otherwise, use a home video recorder to tape yourself reading copy. If a recorder is not available, you may observe yourself in a mirror. Focus on the neck area beneath the chin. Are the muscles of the neck visible when you inhale? Can you see your shoulders move? If either of these is true, you are using your upper chest muscles to inhale.

B) Proper speech production does not begin with the voice being pushed out from the throat or lungs. It begins in the abdominal area. Take a deep breath and sigh. Feel the expansion of the abdomen. Add an audible "ah" sound to the sigh and try to feel the push coming from the abdomen.

C) Various postures and movements force abdominal-diaphragmatic breathing. Try these activities and focus on the movement around the abdominal area, the sides, and the back. Some postures may work better for you than others. In all of them, concentrate on your breathing.

- Bend from the waist at a ninety degree angle, letting your arms and head hang relaxed. Keep your knees slightly flexed. Remain in this position until you can feel your abdominal-diaphragmatic breathing.
- Squat so that your buttocks are resting a few inches above your heels. Remain in this posi-

tion until you can feel the abdominal involvement in your breathing.

- Sit forward in a chair and put your elbows on your knees. Breathe normally and focus attention on the location of the movement.
- Pant like a dog a dozen times. Slow the panting down and notice the abdomen going out as you inhale and in as you exhale.
- Pretend you are Santa Claus and say a strong, "Ho! Ho! Ho!" several times. Notice that the air is pushed from the abdomen.
- Sit up straight on the front edge of a chair. Drop your arms and grab the legs of the chair to lock your shoulders in place so they cannot rise. Push your abdominal area out as you breathe.
- Take a deep inhalation and pretend you are blowing out one hundred candles on a birthday cake. Feel the pressure in the abdominal area as the muscles squeeze to blow out all the candles.
- Tilt your head back and yawn deeply. Feel the movement in your abdominal area. This is an excellent way to relax the throat.

D) One of the best postures for feeling abdominal-diaphragmatic breathing is lying down. Find a comfortable carpet or bed and stretch out on your back. Spread your legs slightly and move your arms away from your body so that there is open space in your armpits. Perform the following activities:

- Close your eyes and concentrate on your breathing.
- Place your right hand on your chest and your left hand on your abdomen. Notice that you can keep your right hand still while your left hand rises and falls with each breath.
- Keeping your hands on your chest and abdomen, take in a deep inhalation, purse your lips,

and blow the air out. Feel your left hand slowly descending as the air is expelled.

- Place a book on your abdomen and watch it rise as you inhale and fall as you exhale.
- Turn over and lie down on your stomach with your hands at your sides. Turn your head sideways and rest your cheek on the bed or floor. Feel your stomach pushing against the surface you are lying on each time you inhale.

E) Working with a partner, put your hand on your partner's abdominal area just above the waist. Ask your partner to inhale and push your hand away. Focus on the movement of the abdominal area. Switch tasks. If either of you has difficulty, forget about breathing and simply push the hand away. Concentrate on moving those muscles, then put an inhalation with the movement.

Breathing Warm-Ups

WARNING: Do not overdo any of the warm-ups in this book. If you feel dizzy or uncomfortable at any time, stop and breathe normally. Do not force or strain.

General Instructions

While doing these warm-ups, use a vocal volume that is appropriate for your broadcast voice or conversation. If the warm-up calls for vocalization, begin the sound immediately. Do not waste any air.

For these warm-ups and for speech, breathing can be done through the mouth. Normally, we breathe through our nose because this filters, warms, and moistens the air. Breathing through the nose is important for normal breathing, but too slow for speech. When speaking, it is appropriate to inhale through the mouth.

These exercises should be done in a standing position. Your posture should be straight, with your knees slightly bent. Try to keep your body as relaxed as possible. As you build your control of exhalation, you will feel the diaphragm rising until it seems to be pushing up into the chest cavity as you reach the end of your vocalization. Do not force vocalization as you deplete your air supply. Always stop if your pitch changes, or if your tone breaks in a glottal fry or a hoarse sound.

You may feel slightly dizzy doing some of these warmups. This is especially true if you are a smoker. Deep abdominal-diaphragmatic inhalations bring large supplies of oxygen to your brain. If your body is not accustomed to this, dizziness may occur. If you become dizzy, sit down and breathe normally for a few seconds. As you continue doing these warm-ups, the dizziness should subside. If it does not, see your physician.

Do not worry about hyperventilating during these warmups. Hyperventilation is fast, shallow breathing that gives a feeling of breathlessness. It is usually associated with anxiety. Hyperventilation causes the carbon dioxide level to drop and lightheadedness, dizziness, or a giddy feeling results. For these exercises, you will be doing the opposite of hyperventilating. You will be breathing slowly, deeply, and with control. Training in controlled breathing is the common treatment for hyperventilation.

You should make these warm-ups part of your daily routine. Practice at least ten minutes a day for several weeks to build breath support. Select the warm-ups you enjoy for your regular routine and add others for variety. You should also begin to use proper breathing whenever you read copy. Using proper breathing will become a habit if you stay aware of your breathing.

1) This is a negative contrast exercise. Take a deep inhalation in the upper chest area. Exaggerate the lifting of the shoulders and tension in the throat. Say an extended "ah" sound. Time the number of seconds you can sustain an "ah." Listen to the quality of the sound. Next take a comfortable abdominal-diaphragmatic breath in a standing position. If you have difficulty with this, go back to the Focus on Breathing section. Once you have inhaled comfortably with the diaphragm, exhale vocalizing "ah." Again, time your "ah" and listen to the quality. With the abdominal-diaphragmatic breath,

your "ah" should sound lower in pitch and vocalization should be longer.

2) Using a child's pinwheel, purse your lips and blow air out making the pinwheel spin. Use your abdominal muscles to sustain a slow, steady spin. Time how long you can make it spin. Try to increase your time as you repeat this exercise.

3) Tear off the corner of a facial tissue. Hold it against a wall with the force of your exhalation. Feel your abdominal area squeezing in as you exhale for as long as possible.

4) With one hand on your abdominal area, take a deep inhalation pushing your hand out. Sustain any of the following vowel sounds on exhalation:

- "ah" as in spa
- "aw" as in caw
- "u" as in two.

Time each vowel production. Stop vocalization when the sound begins to waver or sound weak. At first, your times may be in the ten to fifteen second range. Try to build your control of exhalation by adding a few seconds each time until you can sustain a vowel for twenty to thirty seconds. Keep a record of your progress.

5) Grasp your body so that your fingers touch in the front of your abdominal area and your thumbs reach around toward your back. Take a deep inhalation that pushes your fingers apart. With that breath, vocalize any of the following lists. Make certain that you do not take in any additional small gulps of air. You should be measuring your breath support by exhaling only one inhalation. Keep a record of how far you go each time.

- Repeat the days of the week.
- Count by ones or tens.
- Repeat the months of the year.
- Say the alphabet.

Correct beginning hand
position before and after
exhalation.

Courtesy of WVIR–TV, Charlottesville, VA

Correct hand position after
abdominal-diaphragmatic
inhalation.

Courtesy of WVIR–TV, Charlottesville, VA

6) This exercise is called the "Countdown to Calm Down." If you practice this enough, it will relieve some of the tension that precedes each taping. Establish a habit of using it in the sound booth or for stand-ups. It will break the tension of the day and get you ready to record.

Take a deep abdominal-diaphragmatic inhalation and say, "Broadcast Voice Handbook story, take one." (You would replace this title with your story slug as you make this part of your routine when you begin recording.) Now inhale deeply again, and say, "Three, two, one." Inhale a third time and begin your story. For a practice story opener you can say, "Broadcasters are finding that a few simple breathing exercises can make a difference."

This method of beginning your taping may seem too slow or time-consuming at first. I have found with clients, however, that the four or five seconds needed for the additional breathing are well worth it. Many clients report that they do fewer takes of each piece with this method. They often are pleased with their voice in the first reading after using their countdown time to calm down.

7) Take a deep abdominal-diaphragmatic inhalation and say, "Good evening, I'm (your name) and this is Eyewitness News." Exhale any remaining air. Inhale again and say the phrase twice.

Continue building the number of times you can repeat the phrase on one inhalation, maintaining an appropriate pitch and volume. Keep a record of your progress.

8) Take a good inhalation and read as far as you comfortably can in the following copy. Meaning is not important. Do not try to "sound like a broadcaster." Mark your progress and try to add one more word each time. Avoid dropping into a glottal fry or forcing. If you find it is easy to read the entire selection in one breath, start over and read until you run out of air.

```
A medical researcher says
anyone who drinks five cups of
coffee a day, or more, may be
increasing the chances of
developing lung cancer. The
University of Minnesota
scientist says his study is the
first to implicate coffee by
itself. He also says that if
someone drinks too much coffee
and smokes, the combined
effects may be far worse. But
he says investigators must do
more research.
```

Reprinted with permission from *Writing Broadcast News,* Mervin Block, Bonus Books, Inc., 1987.

9) Marking your copy for breath pauses will make it easier to avoid inappropriate pauses. In Chapter 5, breath pauses are explained as an integral part of the process of marking copy to add stress and intonation to your reading. For practice purposes, the following selections have been marked for pauses. There are many different ways copy can be marked, and this marking may seem awkward to you. Record these anyway to practice, beginning each with your countdown as in Warm-Up 6. The double slash marks indicate a pause with a fairly deep inhalation. The single slash marks mean a quick intake of air (called a catch-breath) or a pause with no breath intake.

Former President Carter arrived
in New York City today to lend
a hand--/in fact, both of
them--/to help rebuild a
burned-out apartment building.//
He came by bus with other
volunteers from his hometown
Baptist church in Plains,
Georgia.// On arrival,/ they
talked over their one-week
project, sponsored by a
religious group.// At the
abandoned building on
Manhattan's Lower East Side,/
Mister Carter,/ an expert
woodworker,/ is going to use
hammer and saw to try to make
the place fit again.//

Seven persons in Wilmington,
Delaware, have pointed to a man
in court and identified him as
the bandit who held them up,/ a
Roman Catholic priest.// But now
another man has come forward,
saying that he committed the
armed robberies,/ not the
priest.// The judge will decide
how to proceed after conferring
today with the prosecutor,/ the
priest/ and the penitent.//

Reprinted with permission from *Writing Broadcast News*, Mervin
Block, Bonus Books, Inc., 1987.

10) Try marking the following selections for breath pauses.
As you found in Warm-Up 9, most double slash marks are found at
periods, and single slashes are at commas, ellipses, dashes, or to
distinguish meaning. Once these are marked, continue the reading
process you established in Warm-Up 9.

Oregon police are searching for a prison escapee who was on board the United Airlines DC-8 that crash-landed in Portland last night. The escapee was being returned by two guards to the Oregon State Prison. 185 persons were on board the plane. In the crash, at least 10 were killed and 45 hurt, five critically. And the escapee apparently escaped again.

Tornadoes and thunderstorms struck the southeast today and caused at least two deaths. Tornadoes in Laurel County, Kentucky, in the London area, overturned mobile homes, toppled trees, battered buildings, peeled off roofs, killed cattle and destroyed or damaged a lot of other property. At least six people there were hurt.

A fire swept through one of the nation's biggest libraries today. The Central Los Angeles Library was damaged severely, and thousands of books were destroyed. 250 firemen fought the fire, and 22 of them were hurt. Firemen were hampered because they tried to hold down the use of water--to minimize water damage to books.

Reprinted with permission from *Writing Broadcast News*, Mervin Block, Bonus Books, Inc., 1987.

Don't ignore voice-impairing illnesses. I have found that most radio news people don't realize how fragile their voices can be, until they lose their voice. The recovery time is typically much longer than expected.

Carolynn Jones
Editor, Bloomberg Business News
Princeton, New Jersey

Don't smoke. It's important to work in a smoke-free environment. And don't strain your voice at sporting events—just clap instead of yell.

Dan Dillon
News Director, KFDI AM/FM
Wichita, Kansas

Develop your own natural vocal quality into a delivery that is easy to listen to. Do not force another vocal quality that's unnatural.

Sheri Haag
News Director, WVVA–TV
Bluefield, West Virginia

Phonation— Using the Vocal Folds Effectively

Whether you are making $9,000 a year as a general assignment reporter in a small market or $3 million as a network anchor, healthy vocal folds (vocal cords) are a prerequisite to your work. It would be ludicrous to think of a concert pianist laying bricks several hours a week. Obviously, most pianists take very good care of their hands. As a broadcaster, you should be equally protective of your vocal mechanism. If you are misusing your voice, you are playing Russian roulette with the part of your anatomy you must depend on for a lifelong career.

This chapter will explain how talking while you are hoarse, coughing, clearing your throat, and shouting can cause physical damage to your vocal folds. More serious damage is caused by smoking, which remains a career and health hazard for broadcasters.

Anatomy of Phonation

Breathing is your best ally as a broadcaster. It provides the energy for speech while relaxing the body. But breathing alone cannot produce speech. In order for sound to be produced, the air from the lungs must be altered to create sound waves. This is called **phonation**. When we speak, we alter air in several ways, but the most important alteration involves the vocal folds.

The vocal folds are folds of muscle that are located within your larynx (Adam's apple). Their position varies from a fully open V-formation that allows air to flow through unimpeded, to a closed position formed when the sides of the V come together to create a valve in our throats (see Figure 4). This valving is the primary purpose of the vocal folds, not speech. The vocal folds protect our lungs from foreign matter by closing off the trachea when food or liquid comes down the pharynx (see Figure 1). Since the pharynx splits into two tubes—the trachea, that goes to the lungs, and the esophagus, that goes to the stomach—this valve is very important. Without the vocal folds, our lungs would be unprotected, and food and liquid could go into our lungs when we swallow, resulting in asphyxiation. Our vocal folds keep us alive by protecting our lungs.

It is easy to feel your vocal folds working. Slide your fingers down the front of your neck until you reach your larynx, which will feel like a protrusion directly beneath your chin. You are feeling the thyroid cartilage, which is a shield-like structure that protects the vocal folds. With your fingers on your larynx make a sustained "e" sound, and you will feel vibrations. Swallow and feel the larynx rising up in the throat. Yawn and you will feel the larynx moving downward. All of this movement is controlled by an intricate system of muscles in your throat.

The entire structure of the larynx or voice box is an alteration of the top two cartilage rings of the trachea (see Figure 1). These rings have altered to protect the vocal folds and to allow them to open and close. The vocal folds are delicate tissues covered with mucous (see Figure 4). Of all our vocal mechanisms, these structures are the most delicate and the most vulnerable.

Most mammals have similar valve systems in their throats to protect their lungs. Other animals' brains and oral structures are

Figure 4
High Speed Photography of Human Vocal Folds Progressing from
Inhalation (upper left) to Voicing (lower right)

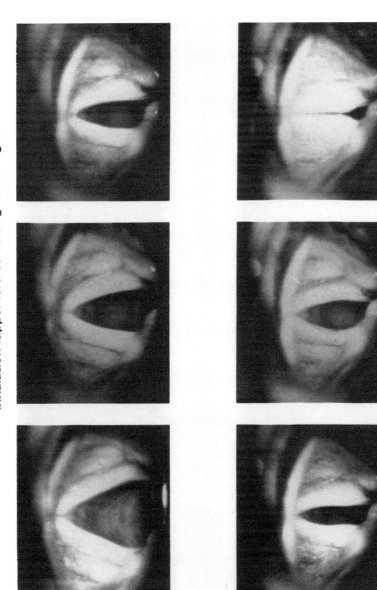

Courtesy of AT & T Archives

not refined enough, however, to produce speech. Cats can meow and dogs bark, but our speech is far more intricate than anything even apes or chimpanzees can produce.

The larynx is arranged in some animals so that they can swallow and smell at the same time to protect themselves while eating. Humans have lost that ability. We cannot inhale while swallowing because our lungs are completely sealed off as a protective measure by the closure of the vocal folds.

We share an important laryngeal attribute with other mammals, however. This is called the glottal effort closure reflex. To feel this reflex, put your palms together and push hard against your hands. To build up pressure to push, you probably closed your vocal folds and trapped air in your lungs. This gives you more upper body strength than you would have with an open airway. Push your hands together and continue breathing as you are pushing, and you will feel much less power.

The primary purposes of the vocal folds are to give us the upper body strength we need and to protect the lungs from foreign matter. When we speak, we are using a life support function that we have adapted to another use.

How Sound Is Produced

To produce sound, we exhale air from the lungs. The brain signals the vocal folds, which are open for normal breathing, to come together to prepare to produce sound. The air builds pressure under the closed vocal folds. When appropriate pressure has built up, the folds are pushed apart. They are then sucked together to block the air again (see Figure 4). This process continues and produces a fluttering effect that alternately blocks the air and lets it pass. This causes the air molecules to be condensed and rarefied, which creates a sound wave. The sound wave can be heard when the altered movement of air forces our eardrum to move at the same frequency as the sound wave.

To experience a process similar to phonation, blow up a balloon and stretch the mouth of the balloon. The air pressure from the balloon will cause the latex at the stretched mouth to flutter, producing a high-pitched squeak. This is caused by the latex being alternately sucked together and pushed apart. Your vocal folds operate much like the mouth of the balloon as they are pulled together and pushed apart to produce sound waves.

Sound waves produced at the vocal folds are measured in cycles per second (cps). A cycle is a complete opening and closing of the vocal folds. Middle C, for example, is 256 cps. These delicate tissues move very rapidly for speech and are vulnerable to misuse.

Common Vocal Problems

To produce sound, the vocal folds must be able to come together as a valve. All the problems associated with phonation involve alteration of the folds, which prevents them from closing effectively. The problems range from a fairly innocuous sore throat to laryngeal cancer. Fortunately, the voice lets us know fairly quickly if there is something wrong in the throat. Pain, hoarseness, and a persistent feeling of a lump in the throat are all signs of a problem.

Hoarseness

The most obvious symptom of a vocal problem is usually hoarseness. It may result from something as simple as a common cold. Hoarseness sounds like a rough, husky, coarse voice. The voice may be lower in pitch than normal and may crack or break as you speak. Any swelling, thickening, or growth on the vocal folds can produce a hoarse voice. Think again of the mouth of a balloon being stretched tightly together. If the latex has a bump in it or is thickened, the closure cannot take place. This is what happens when the folds are swollen or a growth exists.

It is impossible to tell from the sound of your voice whether your hoarseness is caused by a simple swelling, or a benign (noncancerous) or cancerous growth. This is why one of the seven warning symptoms of the American Cancer Society is a nagging cough or hoarseness. In general, if you are hoarse for more than two weeks you should see a doctor. Using a procedure called indirect laryngoscopy, an ear, nose, and throat doctor can look at your vocal folds by inserting something similar to a dentist's mirror in the back of your mouth. Looking down at your folds, the doctor can see what is preventing proper closure.

Laryngitis

A common cause of hoarseness is laryngitis, which in most cases is an acute infection that may be accompanied by a sore throat and fever. This infection usually does not last long, and once the virus is gone your voice returns to normal. Laryngitis changes the healthy pink-colored vocal folds to swollen red tissues.

Chronic laryngitis is a more complex condition caused by vocal misuse. Repeated bouts of laryngitis unaccompanied by fever or sore throat may indicate continued misuse of the vocal mechanism. If your hoarseness is usually worse in the morning when you get up, and you cough frequently, you may suffer from chronic laryngitis. This type of laryngitis requires work with a speech professional to change vocal habits.

In either type of laryngitis the worst thing to do is to continue trying to talk as usual. It is very easy to damage the vocal folds when the tissues are reddened and swollen as they are with laryngitis. When you are hoarse, you should talk as little as possible.

Continuing to talk while hoarse creates what has often been called the **vicious circle of vocal abuse.** You are hoarse, so you try even harder to talk, which makes you even hoarser, and on and on. Not many of us would run a marathon with tight shoes and continue running the next day despite the blisters and callouses that had developed. All too many broadcasters, however, insist they can go on the air with a hoarse voice. By doing so, they are damaging their vocal folds in the same way you would damage your feet by running when they are red and swollen. Hoarseness should be taken very seriously. Talking while you are hoarse can have long-lasting effects and may cause permanent damage.

Vocal rest is the best treatment for laryngitis. If you must talk, use a breathy voice, not a whisper (see Focus on Phonation). For whispering, the vocal folds are held tightly together and sound is produced through a limited opening. This forces the swollen tissue to be held tightly, causing more abrasion. As an example of a breathy voice, think about a sexy voice like that of Marilyn Monroe, Bo Derek, or Zsa Zsa Gabor. The vocal folds are held open and re-laxed, and air comes through the folds without closure of the folds.

If you become hoarse, you can depend on having to rest your voice. It is much healthier for your throat to take time off when you first become hoarse, rather than allowing the condition to get worse through the **vicious circle of vocal abuse** over several days. It is like the old saying, pay me now or pay me later. At some point, you are going to have to rest your throat. Since the vocal folds are so important to your career, I suggest you take time off and rest when you first feel hoarseness developing.

If you must work while you are hoarse, you should limit your talking. If you are a radio news person and must do hourly spot news, try to remain silent between your broadcasts. Get an assistant to make phone calls for you and to go out in the field. Also limit your talking when you are not at work. All of this will help, but if at all possible, take a day off to rest your voice completely.

Take hoarseness seriously. Remember that you are dealing with two delicate pieces of tissue, and abuse of these tissues can cause permanent damage to your body and your career. I have heard incredible stories from clients about bad advice they have been given. One client said that he was not only encouraged to go on the air when hoarse, but was told that shouting with a hoarse voice would lower his pitch. Bad advice like that could easily end his career as a broadcaster. Having healthy vocal folds should be your top priority, and hoarseness is always a sign that your voice is not working correctly.

Vocal Nodules and Polyps

Continued misuse of your voice when you are hoarse may result in vocal nodules (nodes). If swelling is present in the larynx, as it would be with laryngitis, a thickening of the tissue may occur. If you continue to talk, small wart-like growths the size of a pinhead can develop. These nodules are generally on both sides of the vocal folds (bilateral) and are often directly opposite each other (see Figure 5). The nodules may continue to enlarge, and if vocal abuse continues, speech production may become very difficult.

Figure 5

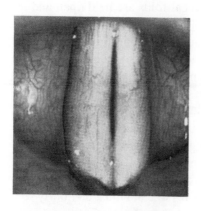

Normal vocal folds (white structures) seen during sound production. Note that healthy vocal folds have a pearly white color and sharp, well-defined contacting surfaces.

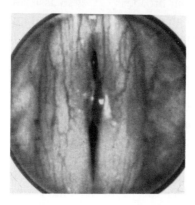

Vocal nodules on both vocal folds. These lesions result from vocal abuse and cause incomplete closure, irregular margins, and added mass to the vocal folds. These contribute to breathiness, hoarseness, lowered pitch, and sometimes roughness in the voice.

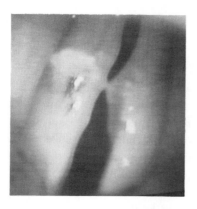

Vocal fold polyp resulting from vocal abuse in an 18-year-old acting student. Note the irregularities and swelling in the mucosa on the non-lesioned (left) vocal fold.

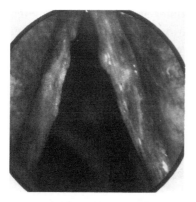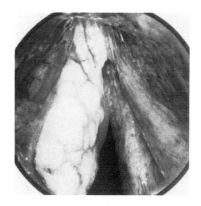

Two laryngoscopic views of the vocal folds in long term smokers. Note that this habit can result in inflammation, architectural changes and the possible development of cancerous lesions on the vocal folds.

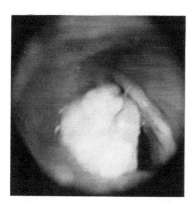

Laryngoscopic view of a large benign tumor of the vocal fold (cottonball structure) found in a 28-year-old woman who was first examined after experiencing hoarseness for three months. This case emphasizes the need to receive medical evaluation of hoarseness that persists for longer than 2 weeks.

Figures provided with the compliments of the Memphis Voice Care Center, a comprehensive multidisciplinary medical specialty clinic dedicated solely to the care of voice and voice-related problems. Through medical treatment, long-range vocal management planning, and continued vocal education, the Center helps patients keep their voices in top shape.

The vocal symptoms for nodules are similar to laryngitis. The voice is hoarse, low-pitched, and may lack sufficient volume. These symptoms do not go away, however, as they would with acute laryngitis.

Nodules are most common in adult women who speak with a tense, loud voice. The typical candidate for vocal nodules is socially aggressive, talks a lot, and is often in tense situations. All of these characteristics are common traits of broadcasters. The voice may have been high-pitched, but it progresses to a low pitch as the nodules get larger. Nodules or nodes are also common in public speakers, singers, and young children (screamer's nodes).

Vocal nodules develop from a combination of overtaxing the voice and incorrect use of the vocal mechanism. Many singers reportedly have numerous operations to remove vocal nodules. Harry Belafonte, for instance, whose singing is characterized by a staccato, explosive use of the voice, reportedly had such surgery. This type of vocal production is called **glottal attack,** and results from an intense build-up of air under the closed vocal folds that is allowed to explode out, causing trauma to the tissues.

Vocal polyps are similar to nodules (see Figure 5), but they are usually only on one fold (unilateral). The vocal symptoms of hoarseness and low pitch are the same as for nodules. Unlike nodules, however, vocal polyps may occur from a single traumatic vocal event. This is why it is so important not to scream at a football game or yell across the newsroom. Even an overly vigorous cough or a forceful clearing of your throat can cause a polyp. One loud burst of sound can abuse the vocal folds enough to cause hemorrhaging. Fluid fills the sac caused by the hemorrhage, which produces a polyp.

When broadcasting, remember that an increase in volume may be harmful to your vocal folds. Talk at a conversational level when on-air. The microphone is only a few inches from your mouth, and that should be your point of focus for your volume. There is usually no need to talk louder, even in very noisy conditions.

Contact Ulcers

Another benign lesion that can develop on the vocal folds is a contact ulcer. This condition is caused by using a tense voice that has a hard glottal attack. The muscular tension used for this type of voice causes the cartilage near the vocal folds to create an ulcer.

Contact ulcers are most often found in hard-driving middle-aged men. Their voices usually begin as low-pitched with some glottal fry sounds. Broadcasters who lower their pitch unnaturally are good candidates for contact ulcers.

Unlike vocal nodules or polyps, contact ulcers usually cause pain in the throat, neck, or even in the ears during swallowing. The person may feel a tickle or lump in the throat. The voice may progress from being strong and forceful to breathy. The breathy voice is used after the ulcers are present to avoid the pain from forceful closure of the vocal folds.

Contact ulcers may be aggravated by gastrointestinal problems. A condition called gastric reflux may aggravate the ulcers in the larynx. **Gastric reflux** occurs when liquid comes up from the stomach during sleep. This liquid may enter the pharynx and move into the laryngeal area, causing irritation to the vocal folds. Avoid heavy evening meals, and do not eat at least two hours before going to sleep to avoid gastric reflux.

Treatment for Vocal Nodules, Polyps, and Ulcers

The good news about all of the benign conditions described above is that they may not require surgery, and they do not appear to be pre-malignant conditions. They are caused by vocal misuse; when the misuse goes away so does the condition. New diagnostic procedures and equipment as well as research have shown that most of these conditions will completely disappear when the voice is used correctly.

Dr. Joshua Oppenheim, an ear, nose, and throat specialist (otolaryngologist) in the Washington, D.C., area, reports that 90 percent of his patients with nodules, polyps, or ulcers do not require surgery. Often, though, work with a speech pathologist to learn proper vocal production is necessary. This work might last from six months to a year in some cases, and involves reducing tension in the larynx and learning to talk with a relaxed voice. Medical treatment is often necessary to control gastric reflux.

If you remain hoarse for more than two weeks, the first step is to get a proper diagnosis. An otolaryngologist might use indirect laryngoscopy or a newer technique called videostroboscopy. This technique involves the use of a video camera and a strobe light. By projecting the strobe light down the throat and timing its flash, the video camera shows the vibrations of the vocal folds as a wavelike movement. This technique allows physicians to view the size and type of the vocal fold problem as well as the resulting interruption in the vibration. Dr. Oppenheim has observed that this equipment allows for a much more precise diagnosis.

If you are having vocal problems, seek a specialist with the latest equipment. Also, always get a second opinion if you are advised to have surgery to remove a benign lesion. In the past, surgery was often recommended, but, as has been pointed out, it may be unnecessary or inappropriate. Surgery is still required in some instances to cure vocal fold lesions that do not respond well to medical or speech therapy, but a second opinion is always appropriate.

Cancer of the Larynx

All vocal problems are not as easily treated as nodules, polyps, and ulcers. Laryngeal cancer requires surgery or radiation, and is a life-threatening condition. The American Cancer Society reports that laryngeal cancer strikes approximately 12,000 persons in the United States each year and causes 3,800 deaths.

As with the benign conditions described above, hoarseness is usually the first symptom of laryngeal cancer, which most often begins as a growth on the vocal folds (see Figure 5). Other symptoms may be a change in pitch, a sense of discomfort or lump in the throat, coughing, difficulty or pain in breathing or swallowing, and earache. Since these symptoms can also signal benign conditions, it is important to have them diagnosed by a physician if they persist for more than two weeks.

The impact of laryngeal cancer on a broadcaster's voice can be profound. Even the nonsurgical technique of radiation therapy can affect the sound of the voice. Surgery to remove a cancerous growth usually affects vocal production significantly. If a laryngectomy is required, the voice is completely lost when the larynx is removed. Following the surgery, the patient breathes through a tracheostoma, a hole made in the lower front of the neck. This is necessary because the important valve provided by the vocal folds has been removed, and the path to the lungs is unprotected. During the surgery it is necessary to block off the trachea permanently from the mouth, and channel breathing out the tracheostoma. In addition to losing the capability of normal vocal production, laryngectomy patients are also physically weaker because they no longer have the glottal effort closure reflex explained earlier in this chapter.

Smoking and Cancer

Unlike nodules, polyps, or ulcers, laryngeal cancer is not caused from vocal misuse. The most common cause of laryngeal cancer is cigarette smoking (see Figure 5). In fact, the American Cancer Society reports that almost all those who develop cancer of the larynx use or have used tobacco. Cigarettes have chemicals that directly irritate the vocal folds when being inhaled and exhaled. Alcohol consumption is another important risk factor. People who smoke *and* drink are at highest risk of cancer.

In addition, smoking is the primary factor in oral cancer which, like laryngeal cancer, can have devastating effects on a broadcaster. According to the American Cancer Society, oral cancer strikes approximately 29,600 persons in the United States each year, causing 7,925 deaths. The death rate from oral cancer is about four times higher for smokers than for nonsmokers. Pipe and cigar smokers may develop oral cancer even if they do not inhale smoke into their lungs.

If those cancers are not enough reason to avoid smoking, lung cancer should be. Smoking has been shown to have a direct connection to lung cancer. The American Cancer Society says that smoking is responsible for eighty-seven percent of lung cancers. They expect 172,000 new cases in 1994 and 153,000 deaths. A person who smokes two packs a day is twenty-five times more likely to die of lung cancer than a nonsmoker.

The dangers of smoking are not limited to broadcasters who smoke. The EPA estimates that environmental tobacco smoke (inhaling smoke from someone else's cigarette) causes nearly three percent of the annual lung cancer deaths per year. This amounts to almost 4,000 persons who die from lung cancer caused from others' cigarettes. The American Cancer Society has found that nonsmokers exposed to twenty or more cigarettes a day at home or work had twice the risk of developing lung cancer. In addition, involuntary smokers suffer more colds, bronchitis, chronic coughs, ear infections, and have reduced lung function.

To summarize the devastating effects of smoking, the American Cancer Society reports in its "Cancer Facts and Figures" for 1994 that cigarette smoking is the single main cause of cancer mortality in the United States. Smoking is directly related to 1,147 deaths *per day* in this country. Compare this to scheduled airline flight fatalities, which totalled only thirty-three *per year* for 1992 (reported by the National Transportation Safety Board), and you begin to understand the significance.

When I speak to groups of broadcasters, I tell them that smoking is just plain stupid if you value your career and your life. The evidence is overwhelming and irrefutable. It is not even a good gamble. If you smoke, the odds are that you will develop vocal problems. Why spend years training to be the best broadcaster you can be, only to defeat yourself by smoking?

Do not admire the classic "smoker's voice." Smokers generally do have a lower-pitched voice, but that is because of the trauma smoking causes to the vocal folds. Incredibly, I was told of a news director who advised the women in his shop to smoke because it would lower their pitch. That advice is the equivalent of telling someone to drive while drunk because he or she will be more relaxed. The effects can be deadly.

Remember the danger of environmental smoke as well. Campaign for a smokeless newsroom. We now have smoke-free airline flights, offices, and restaurants. CNN company policy prohibits smoking in all its newsrooms. Insist on the same for your newsroom.

The once common image of the smoke-filled newsroom should be history. Far too many broadcasters, including Edward R. Murrow, have died from smoking-related illnesses. Ed Bliss, Murrow's writer at CBS Radio, reports that Murrow smoked three to four packs of unfiltered Camels a day. A former Murrow writer advised Bliss to never use adjectives in his copy and always carry a fresh pack of Camels for Murrow. Murrow died of lung cancer at the age of fifty-seven. All the facts about smoking that are now common knowledge were not available thirty years ago. Broadcasters today should avoid all contact with tobacco smoke.

Taking Care of Your Voice

In addition to avoiding tobacco smoke, there are other steps you can take to have a healthy voice. Luckily, vocal hygiene and basic good health often go hand in hand.

Coughing

Straining the voice in any way has a harmful effect on the vocal folds. Perhaps the most common vocal abuse is coughing. When we cough, we build up tremendous air pressure under the vocal folds. The air moves up the trachea very rapidly after being forcefully exhaled by a push from the abdominal muscles. This blast of air is intended to blow any obstruction out of our throat. This might be mucous, if we have a cold, or a piece of food that has started down toward the laryngeal area. When we cough, the air leaving the lungs is moving at close to supersonic speeds. The folds vibrate explosively, which is what is needed to clear the throat.

The force that makes a cough work may also damage the delicate throat tissue. Excessive coughing can be harmful to the vocal folds because of the forceful closure it causes. The folds may begin to swell and eventually become thickened. Any cold or allergy should be controlled to limit the need for coughing.

In certain instances, a blast of air similar to that of a cough can save a person's life. The Heimlich Maneuver (taught by the American Red Cross and the American Heart Association as part of CPR instruction) involves forcing air through the trachea to dislodge food or objects totally blocking the trachea. When foreign matter is caught in the vocal folds, the person cannot make a sound. The universal sign for choking is to grab the throat area; a person is unable to cough, speak, or breathe. During the Heimlich Maneuver, the person's abdominal area is compressed forcefully. The diaphragm rises, and the effect is as if you slammed the handles of a bellows closed. Anything stuck in the tube of the bellows would be blasted out. In a similar manner, food stuck in someone's throat may actually fly across the room if the Heimlich Maneuver is done correctly.

Throat Clearing

Throat clearing can also be harmful if done excessively. As when coughing, clearing your throat causes your folds to vibrate explosively. This can cause swelling and may lead to the development of polyps or nodules on the vocal folds. Clearing your throat is like a small cough, and it can become a habit. Some people feel the need to clear their throat repeatedly through the day. Try to be aware of how often you clear your throat and keep it to a minimum. You may have to ask a friend to observe how many times you clear your throat, since this action is often unconscious.

Allergies are often a factor in throat clearing. If you find yourself clearing your throat a great deal, it might be helpful to have yourself tested for different allergies. An allergy to certain foods or substances may be causing your discomfort.

One food group that commonly makes people clear their throats and cough is milk products. If you like to drink milk in the morning or have cereal for breakfast, you may find yourself clearing your throat all morning. Milk products establish a condition in our throats conducive to the development of mucous. If you avoid milk products before going on air, you will find your throat much clearer. Save the consumption of milk products for after your on-air work if you find they contribute to coughing or throat clearing.

Loud Speech

Vocal nodules and polyps are linked with overly loud speech. For loud speech, the vocal folds come together very forcefully. They open slower but close much more quickly.

Most broadcasters are aware of their volume on the air because of the advice they receive from engineers. What they may not monitor, however, is the volume of their speech at other times. Many people with slight hearing loss, for instance, consistently speak too loudly.

Newsroom noise may contribute to loud speech.
Courtesy of KSL-TV, Salt Lake City, UT

Another condition that may cause loud speech is a noisy newsroom without an intercom. All too often I find myself in a newsroom where police scanners are blaring, several monitors are on, and ten or twenty people are trying to talk on the phone or to others in the newsroom. As calls come in, I hear on-air broadcasters shouting over this chaos to tell someone else to pick up the phone.

For good vocal hygiene, you should limit your talking in noisy places. This includes the newsroom described above as well as cars or vans, airplanes, trains, or anywhere that requires an increase in volume. And, of course, avoid shouting at sports or music events. Remember that you are making your living on those two little muscles in your throat, and you must take care of them.

Vocal Hydration

The vocal folds are covered with mucous. This moist condition is important to aid in proper vocal fold closure. If the throat is dry, the folds are more likely to be damaged because they lack the appropriate mucous to protect them. Any condition that dehydrates body tissues also dries out the throat.

Often reporters' assignments require broadcasting from noisy locations such as Dan Rather faced in Tiananmen Square during the Chinese pro-democracy uprising.

Courtesy of CBS News.

Excessive mouth breathing can dry out the throat. It is appropriate to breathe through your mouth when you are talking. At other times, breathing should be through the nose so that the air can be filtered, warmed, and moisturized before it goes into the laryngeal area. If you have any blockage in the nose that causes mouth breathing, it should be corrected. In addition, you should avoid breathing through your mouth when you are asleep. Sleeping on your back will often cause mouth breathing. Since this sleeping posture may cause back pain as well, it should be avoided. Sleeping on your side with your mouth closed is best.

If you have a cold or a stuffy nose, decongestants will help open a blocked nasal cavity, but they accomplish this by drying out the tissues. If the nose is dried out, the throat is also. When you have a cold it is difficult to avoid drying the throat, since you will most likely be breathing through your mouth if you do not take a decongestant. This is one of the reasons why it is so important to drink plenty of liquids and inhale steam when you have cold symptoms.

Forced air heating and air conditioning are used in most homes and newsrooms as well as on airplanes and trains. This dry air also contributes to a dry throat. If you live and work in this type of environment or in an excessively dry climate, a humidifier should be used (see Chapter 7). This pumps moisture into the air to lessen the harmful drying effects of the forced air. You can also inhale moisture by using a facial steamer, which gives you the added advantage of moisturizing your facial tissues as well. Simply inhaling steam from a pot of boiling water will also help your throat. (Make certain it does not burn your throat or skin.)

One important chemical that takes water out of the body by acting as a diuretic on the kidneys is caffeine (or technically xanthine, which includes the chemicals in tea and cocoa). One cup of coffee will not have a tremendous effect on your tissues, but if you combine that with other sources of caffeine (see Table 1), you can easily suffer from its usage.

It is easy for caffeine consumption to become excessive. Looking at Table 1, you will see that if you consumed three cups of coffee, a glass of iced tea, an ounce of chocolate, a Diet Coke, and two Excedrin tablets in one day you would be in the range of 610 milligrams of caffeine. Since caffeine also stimulates the central nervous system and your heart, excessive amounts are not good for your throat or your body. Most recommendations suggest no more than two cups of coffee a day or around 200 milligrams. Caffeine does give you a sense of alertness, but as Chapter 1 explained, that can be achieved in healthier ways through proper breathing.

Alcohol also works as a diuretic. It robs your tissues of needed moisture. Dehydration may be the cause of the hangover headache. The classic symptoms of dry mouth and excessive thirst the morning after signal the degree of dehydration that has occurred. In addition, chronic alcohol abuse is linked with laryngeal and oral cancer. For a healthy body and voice, alcohol consumption should be limited.

The best way to combat the drying effects of alcohol, caffeine, and environmental factors is by drinking as much water as possible. Based on the advice of several doctors and nutritionists, I now recommend that clients drink one-half ounce of water per pound of body weight every day. This adjusts water intake for body size. It is much healthier to keep a mug filled with water on your

Table 1
Caffeine Content of Beverages, Foods, and Common Drugs

	Milligrams of Caffeine
Coffee (5 oz.)	
Brewed, drip method	115
Brewed, percolator	80
Instant	65
Decaffeinated, brewed	3
Decaffeinated, instant	2
Tea (5 oz.)	
Brewed, major U.S. brands	40
Brewed, imported brands	60
Instant	30
Iced (12 oz.)	70
Cocoa beverage (5 oz.)	4
Chocolate milk beverage (8 oz.)	5
Milk chocolate (1 oz.)	6
Dark chocolate, semisweet (1 oz.)	20
Baker's chocolate (1 oz.)	26
Chocolate-flavored syrup (1 oz.)	4

Source: FDA, Food Additive Chemistry Evaluation Branch, based on evaluations of existing literature on caffeine levels.

Soft Drinks (12 oz.)	
Sugar-Free Mr. PIBB	58.8
Mountain Dew	54.0
Mello Yellow	52.8
TAB	46.8
Coca-Cola	45.6

	Milligrams of Caffeine
Diet Coke	45.6
Shasta Cola	44.4
Shasta Cherry Cola	44.4
Shasta Diet Cola	44.4
Mr. PIBB	40.8
Dr. Pepper	39.6
Sugar-Free Dr. Pepper	39.6
Big Red	38.4
Sugar-Free Big Red	38.4
Pepsi-Cola	38.4
Aspen	36.0
Diet Pepsi	36.0
Pepsi Light	36.0
RC Cola	36.0
Diet Rite	36.0
Kick	31.2
Canada Dry Jamaica Cola	30.0
Canada Dry Diet Cola	1.2

Source: Institute of Food Technologists (IFT), April 1983, based on data from the National Soft Drink Association, Washington, D.C. IFT also reports that there are at least 68 flavors and varieties of soft drinks produced by 12 leading bottlers that have no caffeine.

	Milligrams of Caffeine
Prescription Drugs	
Cafergot (for migraine headaches)	100
Fiorinal (for tension headaches)	40
Soma Compound (muscle relaxant)	32
Darvon Compound (pain relief)	32.4
Nonprescription Drugs	
Weight-Control Aids	
Dex-A-Diet II	200
Dexatrim Extra Strength	200
Dietac capsules	200
Maximum Strength Appedrine	100
Prolamine	140

	Milligrams of Caffeine
Alertness Tablets	
Nodoz	100
Vivarin	200
Analgesic/Pain Relief	
Anacin, Maximum Strength	
Anacin	32
Excedrin	65
Midol	32.4
Vanquish	33
Diuretics	
Aqua-Ban	100
Maximum Strength Aqua-Ban	
Plus	200
Permathene H2 Off	200
Cold/Allergy Remedies	
Coryban-D capsules	30
Triaminicin tablets	30
Dristan Decongestant tablets &	
Dristan A-F Decongestant	
tablets	16.2
Duradyne-Forte	30

Source: FDA's National Center for Drugs and Biologics. FDA also notes that caffeine is an ingredient in more than 1,000 nonprescription drug products as well as numerous prescription drugs.

desk rather than coffee. Drink from it all day to keep your body and throat hydrated. Avoid ice water as it may constrict the muscles in the throat.

If you feel the need to drink warm liquids, try to avoid caffeine. You can drink decaffeinated coffee or tea, herbal tea, or warm water with lemon. Singers try spraying their throats with various solutions to increase moisture, but this is not necessary if you drink plenty of liquids. In addition, be aware that gargling may dry and stress the vocal fold area since you are blowing air up forcefully to gargle. The best way to have a healthy, well-hydrated throat is to drink plenty of water.

The Ideal Newsroom

I often joke with news directors that my ideal newsroom would have sound booths set up for standing, a standing anchor desk, no smoking signs everywhere, spring water dispensers instead of coffee pots, intercoms to avoid yelling, and humidifiers. I am not sure I will see every newsroom making these changes in this century, but as more data becomes available about the harmful behaviors mentioned above, changes will occur.

Pitch

We not only produce sound with our vocal folds, but we also have the ability to alter the pitch or musical note of that sound. We alter pitch by increasing or decreasing the vibrations per second of the vocal folds. We can go from middle C (256 cps) to high C (512 cps) and cover all the pitches in between. Sing this eight tone (one octave) scale "do-re-mi-fa-sol-la-ti-do." This is accomplished by a subtle shortening and lengthening of the vocal folds.

The V-shaped opening of the vocal folds is positioned with the folds connecting in the front of our throat. The apex/bottom of the V is directly behind the thyroid cartilage (Adam's apple). The two ends of the folds that move are toward the back of the trachea. They are each connected to a triangular-shaped arytenoid cartilage. These cartilages can pivot, rotate, and tilt backwards or sideways to alter the length of the folds and thus change the pitch.

The pitch we create is determined by the length, thickness, and degree of tension of the folds. Men's voices are generally about one octave lower than women's because men have longer vocal folds (around three-quarters of an inch in men versus one-half inch in women). During childhood, girls and boys have similar pitches. The male larynx, however, goes through an explosion of growth at puberty and nearly doubles in size. During this spurt of growth, boys' voices are very unpredictable, and often produce embarrassing voice breaks.

A healthy voice has a range of about one and one-half octaves. Opera singers expand their range significantly, with men reaching two octaves and women often reaching three. A tenor, for example, might sing from middle C (256 cps) down an octave (128 cps) and up an octave (512 cps). This skill comes from practice and training to expand pitch range.

When we lower our pitch, the arytenoid cartilages move so that the folds become shorter and thicker. Low pitch is produced by short, thick, relaxed folds. For high pitch, the folds are stretched tight, producing thinner, tenser folds. The pitch is determined by the cross-sectional mass. Thick folds move slowly, which produces a low pitch, and thin, tense folds move more rapidly, producing a high pitch.

To achieve this change in pitch, the muscles in the larynx must move. The larynx actually rises in the throat slightly for a high-pitched sound and moves down noticeably for a low pitch. To experience this, put your fingers on your Adam's apple and hum a familiar song such as "Happy Birthday." You will feel the larynx moving as the pitch changes.

It is interesting to watch the head positions of television news reporters and anchors as they change pitch. Many times the head will drop down when the pitch is lowered on a word or phrase. Proponents of the affected "Ted Baxter" voice often lower their chin and compress the neck area before beginning their on-air voice. If you remember Ted on *The Mary Tyler Moore Show,* you know that his conversational voice was much higher-pitched than his on-air voice. The Jim Dial character on the show *Murphy Brown* is another good example of this affected voice.

It is important to note that pitch is accomplished by changing the tension in the throat. A higher pitch is produced by greater tension. If you feel your pitch is consistently too high, it may be because of too much tension in the throat. Think of how your voice sounds when you are relaxed and contented, such as when you first awaken or after a cozy evening by the fire. You might say you have a mellow voice. Compare this to your voice in the sound booth after a frantic day of news coverage. You might characterize both your day and your voice as tense. It is this tension that causes the pitch to rise.

If you feel your voice is too high-pitched, the first step toward improving it is to achieve relaxation in the throat area. Most of us hold our greatest degree of tension in our shoulders and neck area. Relaxing this area is imperative for good vocal production. Using abdominal-diaphragmatic breathing will help a great deal (see Focus on Breathing and Breathing Warm-Ups in Chapter 1). Relaxing your neck by doing simple neck rolls will help as well (see Focus on Phonation, Phonation Warm-Ups, and Appendix D). Be aware that a tense body usually means a tense voice. (For more on relaxation, see Chapter 7.)

Optimum Pitch

Inappropriate habitual pitch can cause vocal abuse. If you are speaking above or below your natural frequency, you are using unnecessary muscular energy, which can result in vocal fatigue and hoarseness. Voice professionals disagree about whether inappropriate pitch can cause vocal nodules, but there is evidence to link excessive low pitch to contact ulcers.

Equally as important to you as a broadcaster is the effect of inappropriate pitch on expressiveness. If you are consistently talking at the low end of your pitch range, you have no room to drop your pitch for emphasis. The same is true of a pitch that is too high.

I rarely see clients who feel their pitch is too low. Most clients complain that their voices are too high-pitched. The questionnaire results in Appendix A confirm that news directors agree. Thirty percent say high pitch is a problem, and less than one percent mention low pitch. (Note that radio and television news directors differ on this.) Many times broadcasters adopt an inappropriately low pitch to compensate for a pitch they feel is too high. They drop their pitch when they go on the air. By doing this, they accomplish a low-pitched sound, but the damage they are doing to their vocal folds becomes apparent. They often complain of vocal fatigue, breathiness, or frequent bouts of hoarseness.

The goal for proper voice production is to talk in your optimum pitch range, which is usually around one-fourth of the way up from the bottom of your range. At your optimum pitch, the muscles of the larynx are functioning best, and your voice is comfortable to use. Pitch changes are easy to produce and require the least effort when you are using your optimum pitch. The most resonant tones are produced at the optimum pitch because it matches the pitch range of the resonators above the larynx (see Chapter 3).

It is difficult in a book such as this to give instructions on how to find your optimum pitch range. That is more appropriately done by a voice coach, singing teacher, or speech pathologist. Suffice it to say, however, that achieving relaxation in the vocal mechanism is always the first step toward finding your optimum pitch range.

Problems that are perceived as pitch problems are often not related to phonation, but to resonance, which is the enrichment of the sound in our vocal cavities. You are not the best judge of whether your voice is too high-pitched. I often find that clients are using the correct pitch but are limiting vocal resonance in such a way that their voice seems high-pitched and thin. These clients need work on resonance, not pitch. (For more on resonance, see Chapter 3.)

Beware of anyone who advises you to lower your pitch. As has been noted, finding your best pitch range is a complicated process, and not something with which to experiment. It should only be done with the guidance of a trained professional.

If you came to me as a client and had a fairly high-pitched voice, I could certainly give you a deeper voice by telling you to drop your pitch an octave. Likewise, I could make you seem taller by telling you to walk on your tiptoes all the time. Both of these activities would produce the desired results, but they would do so at the expense of your muscles. Eventually you would not be able to talk or walk without problems.

In lectures to news directors, I often play a tape of a client who came to me because of vocal fatigue. His conversational voice was relaxed and pleasant. As soon as I handed him a microphone, however, he dropped his voice into an unnaturally low pitch. I finally convinced him his natural pitch was appropriate for the air. The before and after tape I play usually brings laughter because he sounds so much better in his natural pitch range. Everyone wonders why he suffered so long to produce a tense, unnatural, low-pitched voice.

Your goal should be to talk in a relaxed, well-resonated voice that requires the least amount of energy to maintain. Manipulating the muscles in your throat to achieve a voice you or others think sounds better can result in vocal damage. You might have a great voice for a few years, but your career will be limited by the strain you are putting on your vocal mechanism.

Focus on Phonation

Here is a summary of the advice given in this chapter to help you have a healthy voice. These recommendations are important to observe daily, and are especially important if you have a cold or a sore throat.

Ten Recommendations for a Healthy Voice

1) Practice abdominal-diaphragmatic breathing to decrease tension in the laryngeal area.
2) Do not smoke or expose yourself to the smoke of others.
3) Avoid excessive alcohol consumption.
4) Avoid eating at least two hours before you go to bed. Avoid milk products before on-air work.
5) Do not talk loudly or in noisy environments such as airplanes, cars, boats, or sports and music events.
6) Keep your vocal tract moist by drinking one-half ounce of water per pound of body weight a day, using a humidifier or inhaling steam, and avoiding substances and environments that dehydrate. Decaffeinated warm drinks may also be consumed, or hot water with lemon.
7) Avoid mouth breathing except for speech. Limit throat clearing and coughing.
8) If you do become hoarse, limit your talking, and use a breathy voice, not a whisper.
9) Use a pitch that is comfortable and does not cause vocal fatigue.
10) See a physician if hoarseness, pain, or odd sensations in the throat last for more than two weeks.

Relaxation is the key to good phonation. Many of the activities listed below are designed to achieve maximum relaxation in the laryngeal area.

A) A whisper requires a great deal of tension in the vocal folds. They must come together tightly, and sound is produced in a small opening. To feel the tension this requires, imagine you are leading your crew out of a city council meeting. You must get everyone to follow you to the van, but you do not want to disturb the meeting. Whisper loudly, "Come with me, everybody." Whisper this several times and feel the tension in your throat. Now completely relax your throat and attempt to say the same phrase in a breathy voice. Begin with a barely audible sound that feels like the "h" in "hello." For a breathy voice, the vocal folds are left open in their V-shaped position and air rushes over them. The throat remains completely relaxed. The breathy voice will not sound as loud, but the throat will be relaxed. This is the voice you should use when you have any hoarseness or discomfort in your throat.

B) For negative contrast, take a breath using the clavicular muscles, so that the shoulders rise on inhalation. After you have inhaled, hold the breath and feel the tension in your throat. Next, take an abdominal-diaphragmatic breath (see Focus on Breathing in Chapter 1). Hold the breath and compare the degree of tension in the throat. You should feel much less tension with the abdominal-diaphragmatic breath.

C) To feel the larynx moving, put your fingers on your Adam's apple and make an "e" sound as in "bee." Change the pitch of the sound and feel the larynx rise for the higher pitch and move downward for the lower pitch.

D) To compare voiced and voiceless sounds in our language, put your fingers on your Adam's apple. Bring your lips together and make a "p" sound (the initial sound in the word "pot"). Now make a "b" sound (as in "Bob"). You should feel vibrations of the vocal folds for the "b" but not for the "p."

E) If you want to get a feeling of what your optimum pitch might be, sigh deeply with an "ah" sound. This "ah" will usually be in your optimum pitch.

F) To avoid laryngeal tension, you should develop the sense that your voice does not come from your larynx or your mouth, but from your diaphragm in the solar plexus region. Our entire body produces speech. Imagine a bellows with a reed at the end of the neck. All the energy to make that reed vibrate comes from your arms pushing the bellows shut. The reed does not move by itself. In the same way, our voice does not come from the vocal folds, but begins with the breath, which is the energy that produces the movement of the folds. Gaining a sense of body involvement in vocal production can be helpful in eliminating tension and producing the healthiest voice possible. Two authors who have written extensively on body involvement in speech are Kristin Linklater and Arthur Lessac (see Suggested Readings). Their books are recommended. In addition, instruction in the Alexander Technique, tai chi, and yoga can help develop this feeling. Acting classes are also helpful.

Phonation Warm-Ups

Phonation warm-ups are aimed at reducing tension in the laryngeal area. They should be performed until relaxation has occurred. Be careful not to exercise the vocal folds too much since vocal fatigue may occur.

1) Yawning has been used for centuries as a technique to relax the throat. A good yawn relaxes the larynx and throat and brings in a good air supply. Practice yawning for relaxation. Drop the jaw and think of what a good yawn feels like. Yawning is sometimes contagious, so take the opportunity to yawn when you see others doing so. Add a sigh at the end of your yawn to feel your relaxed, open throat. After yawning, say this phrase with the same open throat, "How many hats does Henry have?" Say this several times, trying to preserve the open feeling.

Most of us tend to hold tension in our shoulders, upper back, and neck. To relieve this tension, try these warm-ups. Be careful not to stretch your muscles too much.

2) Clasp your hands behind your back. Squeeze your shoulder blades together and raise your arms slightly, tilting your head back. Hold your arms up for five seconds at the point you feel resistance. Release. Repeat this warm-up until your shoulders and upper back feel relaxed.

3) Place your hands on your shoulders. Rotate your shoulders by bringing your elbows together in front, moving them down, back, and up in a circular movement. Rotate five times in one direction and five times in the opposite direction.

4) Very slowly drop your chin to your chest and roll your head up to your right shoulder. Roll your head back down to your chest and roll your head up to your left shoulder. Bring your chin back down to your chest. Repeat slowly three times. (Do not roll your head back. This may cause neck injuries.)

5) Look straight ahead. Rotate your head slowly and look over each shoulder as if you were signaling an exaggerated "no." Repeat twice.

6) To relax the throat, take a deep abdominal-diaphragmatic breath and exhale an "ah" sound. Inhale again and exhale an "ou" sound as in "you." Inhale a third time and exhale an "m" sound. Feel the resonance in the nasal cavity for the "m."

7) To gain flexibility in pitch, say "one" at your normal pitch level. Now go up one step in pitch and say "two." Go up another step in pitch and say "three." Go back down to your normal pitch with "three, two, one." Now go down in pitch one step and say "two." Go down another step and say "three." Go back up to your normal pitch. This process would look like this:

```
        three three
    two              two
one                  one one                    one
                           two            two
                            three three
```

You might want to trace the steps in pitch in the air with your finger as your voice produces them. Tape recording this and the following warm-up work will help you hear if you are really producing the pitch changes you hope for.

8) Continue pitch work by saying the phrase

```
            up
"My voice is going      in pitch."
"My voice is going      in pitch."
            down
```

Repeat these two phrases until you feel comfortable with your pitch changes.

9) Use this phrase to expand your pitch range:

```
                          up."
                    up
                  up
                up
              up
"I can make my voice go
"I can make my voice go
                  down
                        down
                            down
                              down
                                  down."
```

When doing this warm-up, do not push your voice into an artificially high or low pitch. Going too high or low can cause vocal fatigue and possible abuse. For a falsetto, for example, the vocal folds are pulled excessively tight, and they lose their wave-like motion. As with any unnatural position of the folds, this can be harmful.

10) Sing up the musical scale by singing

```
                  do
                ti
              la
            sol
          fa
        mi
      re
    do
```

Do this until you feel comfortable with these eight tones.

*Voice is critical to a news department . . .
because it is the first indicator an audience has
to gauge whether a reporter knows what he or
she is talking about. . . . If the reporter sounds
young and inexperienced the audience is
immediately put on notice.*

**David Jensch
News Director, KBJR–TV
Duluth, Minnesota**

*Authoritative does not mean speaking in a
low pitch and loud! An authoritative reporter
has command of the story but still
speaks conversationally.*

**Scott Benjamin
News Director, WROC–TV
Rochester, New York**

Resonance— Enriching Speech Sound

When people criticize the quality of a broadcaster's voice, they are usually talking about resonance. The vocal folds generate sound waves, but the resonating cavities enrich and augment the sound. Just as no two people look exactly alike, no two vocal mechanisms are exactly alike. The difference in the shape, size, and resiliency of the resonating cavities makes each voice unique.

Resonance not only gives us each a different voice, but it also allows our voices to be heard. To create sound waves, the vocal folds set air in motion in a wave-like fashion, bursting open and closed. If these sound waves were not resonated, they would produce a faint sound, barely audible to the human ear. The slight movement of air at the vocal folds must be enriched by the air and resonating structures above it in the throat.

Characteristics of Resonance

All sound-producing instruments use resonance to enrich their sounds. A guitar string nailed between two pieces of wood would not make a musical sound that you could hear easily. Plucking that string would produce a very thin, weak sound. Put that string on a guitar, however, and the sound is enriched by the body of the guitar and the air trapped in the body. The sound waves become louder and richer.

Resonance is the ability of one body of molecules to set another body of molecules into the same wave-like motion. These may be air molecules or a solid structure. Notice how solid objects vibrate when there is a loud crash of thunder or an explosion. If you feel a table or wall when this happens, you can feel the molecules moving (vibrating).

Touching a vibrating tuning fork to different surfaces also demonstrates how solid matter resonates sound. A vibrating middle C tuning fork will sound different depending on what you touch it to. The structure of the solid matter determines the quality of the sound you hear. The pitch remains middle C, but the quality changes.

Resonance also results from air molecules being set into motion. Musical wind instruments work on the principle of air chamber resonance. Middle C played on a flute sounds different from the same note played on a tuba because of the resonating qualities of their structures. The same is true of a cello and a violin. The fundamental frequency played may be the same, but the quality we hear is very different.

Anatomy of Vocal Resonance

Our voices work on the same principle as a wind instrument. Sound begins with the vocal folds setting air into motion. These sound waves created at the vocal folds are then resonated in the cavities of the throat, mouth, and nose. The fundamental pitch established at the vocal folds is important, but equally important is the manner is which this pitch is resonated.

Variables of Vocal Resonance

Sound waves react in specific ways depending on the cavities they encounter. The harmonics, or secondary vibrations (overtones), created along with the fundamental pitch are either enriched or damped off (killed) depending on the type of environment they enter. All resonating bodies have a natural frequency at which they resonate best. Consequently, they will damp some harmonics and emphasize the amplitude of those closest to the natural frequency of the resonating body.

A jug band is a good example of this. If you blow over a big jug you hear a deep sound. A small jug produces a high, shrill sound. You may blow over these with the same intensity, but as the air rushes around inside the jug some sound waves are damped and others are emphasized. A larger cavity allows more low-pitched or long sound waves to survive. Smaller cavities damp the long sound waves, and a higher pitch results.

There are four principles of tube or cavity resonance that specifically affect speech. Vocal resonance is affected by:

1) the length of the tube or size of the cavity it passes through (larger cavities resonate lower frequencies),
2) the elasticity of the walls of the tube or cavity (softer, more relaxed surfaces resonate lower frequencies),
3) the size of the lip opening of the tube or cavity (smaller openings resonate lower frequencies),
4) the constriction along the tube or cavity.

These principles apply to the jug band, our speech, and any sound-producing source. Just like the jug band, we can alter the size of our resonating cavities to make our voices sound richer or thinner. We have three basic resonating cavities that affect our vocal sound: the pharynx, oral cavity, and nasal cavity.

Pharynx

The pharynx is a soft-sided, muscular tube about five inches long that begins at the larynx and goes up to the nasal cavity (see Figure 6). You see the back wall of this tube in a mirror when you open your mouth and say "ah." If you think of human resonating cavities as being in an "F" shape, the main, upright line would be the pharynx.

```
P NOSE
H
A MOUTH
R
Y
N
X
```

The pharynx is important for vocal resonance because it gives tube resonance to our voices. Just like the body of a clarinet or any wind instrument, the tube of the pharynx provides air trapped in a cylinder that will vibrate. Like any resonating body, a tube has a natural frequency at which it resonates best. A pipe organ or a xylophone is designed with this in mind. The resonating tubes vary in length corresponding to the notes they are to resonate. The longer tubes resonate the lower frequencies.

Our vocal resonance is affected by the length of our pharynx. A child's pharynx, for example, is short, which works best for higher frequency resonance. Because a child's vocal folds are also short and produce a high-pitched sound, the pharynx is appropriate to resonate a child's voice.

Adult voices sound more resonant if the pharynx is longer and has a greater diameter. For the most part, this is an anatomical feature and not something that can be controlled during speech.

One adjustment in the pharynx that does take place involves the larynx rising for a higher pitched sound and lowering for low-pitched sounds (see Focus on Phonation in Chapter 2). This may be an attempt to match the length of the pharynx with the pitch of the sound. This happens automatically just as the larynx rises and the pharynx constricts when you swallow. I have seen broadcasters,

Figure 6
Resonating Cavities

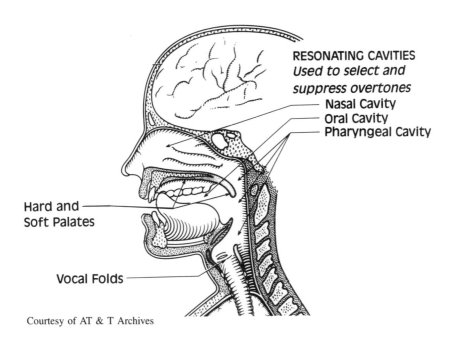

RESONATING CAVITIES
Used to select and
suppress overtones
Nasal Cavity
Oral Cavity
Pharyngeal Cavity

Hard and
Soft Palates

Vocal Folds

Courtesy of AT & T Archives

however, who purposefully constrict their necks by lowering their chins and pushing their heads back. This action seems to lower the pitch, but it increases tension in the throat area and also shortens the pharynx.

The elasticity of the walls of the pharynx also affects the quality of the resonance. A relaxed throat creates the best atmosphere for good resonance. A hard, tense throat may emphasize the higher harmonics of the voice, resulting in a harsh, strident voice. A relaxed throat usually results in a longer, softer pharynx, which produces a mellow, rich voice.

Oral Cavity

Our mouths are our most flexible resonators. We can vary the shape by moving the tongue, jaw, cheeks, and velum (soft palate). The oral cavity is also changed by any addition to the mouth, like dental braces, bridge work, or false teeth. Even tooth bonding slightly changes the resonance characteristics of the oral cavity. The tonsils lie directly behind the oral cavity in the pharangeal area, and their removal greatly changes the shape of the resonating cavities.

The tongue is a major factor in oral resonance. It fills the bottom of the mouth and continues down to form the front of the pharynx. Manipulating the tongue helps us articulate our sounds and resonate them. For the "ee" sound, for example, we raise and tense the tongue to fill part of our oral cavity. Compare the formation of the "ee" sound to "ah."

The vowels in our language are produced mainly by adjusting the shape of our oral cavity. We change its size to accentuate certain harmonics and reduce others. The same pitch, therefore, can sound like an "ee" or an "ah" based on our manipulation of the oral cavity that changes the resonance (see Focus on Resonance).

Anyone who can talk like Donald Duck knows that this is accomplished by bunching the tongue in the back of the mouth to limit the size of the resonating cavity. Likewise, a childish voice results from small resonating cavities. Experiment with this feeling by saying your name first with the tongue down and then with it pushed high up in the mouth toward the hard palate. By making the oral cavity smaller, you reduce the size of the resonating cavity. Just like the sound coming from the small jug, the voice sounds higher pitched.

Unfortunately, many speakers have developed a habit of bunching the tongue up in the mouth while speaking. This produces the thin, immature-sounding voice that plagues some female (and occasionally male) broadcasters, and contributes to the nasality or palatal production of certain sounds in the midwestern and New York dialects. For both these problems, opening the mouth more and lowering the tongue is the key to improvement (see Resonance Warm-Ups).

The jaw also plays an important role in oral resonance. Good flexibility of the jaw helps create a better opening. It is not surprising that the jaw often causes difficulties with resonance. The closing muscles of the jaw are some of the strongest in our body because they are designed for chewing. We often hold tension in the jaw area and clench our mouths shut. Many people do this while sleeping, and they may even grind their teeth at night. If you tend to hold your mouth tightly closed and clench your teeth at night, it is difficult to relax the jaw for speaking. You should concentrate on exercises to relax the jaw (see Resonance and Articulation Warm-Ups in this chapter and Chapter 4).

For good oral resonance, the jaw should be relaxed and free-moving. Eliminating tension from the neck area before speaking is important (see Appendix D and Phonation and Resonance Warm-Ups in this chapter and Chapter 2). Proper abdominal-diaphragmatic breathing assists in maintaining a relaxed throat (see Breathing Warm-Ups in Chapter 1). It is also a good idea to consciously try to keep space between your teeth during the day. Resist clenching your teeth. This will help your voice sound better and reduce tension in your vocal mechanism.

It is not advisable to smile when speaking. When you smile, you pull the cheek muscles back and tense them. You also have a wider mouth opening. One of the characteristics of resonance is that the smaller the mouth opening, the lower the frequencies resonate. Spreading the lips in a smile increases the size of the mouth opening and can contribute to the production of a high-pitched, strident sound. It is not accidental that most beauty pageant contestants sound alike. Their perpetual smiles have a negative affect on their resonating cavities.

You should make the most of your mouth as a resonating cavity since it is the most flexible resonator. It is amazing what can be accomplished when the mouth is improved as a resonating cavity. When clients come to me saying they want to lower their pitch, what they are usually seeking is more resonance. Remember, the flute and the tuba can play exactly the same pitch, but it sounds completely different. This difference is created by changing the resonance of the sound after it leaves the mouthpiece of the musical instrument. All of us can change our vocal sound as well by resonating it differently.

Nasal Cavity

The nasal cavity is another resonating area that can change our sound significantly. We all have heard the whining, honking sound of someone with a nasal voice. This type of voice is unpleasant because the nasal cavity is not as good at resonating as the oral cavity.

Our nasal cavities are the least controllable of the resonating areas. The nasal cavity is about four inches long and is divided by the septum, which is a wall of cartilage and bone running from our nostrils to the soft palate. The septum extends upward from the roof of the hard palate to the bottom of the brain cavity.

The septum and the mucous in the nasal cavity tend to damp low-frequency sound waves. A sound that would be full and resonate coming out of our mouths becomes high and whiny coming from our noses. The frequency of the sound may be the same when it enters the cavities, but the size of the available resonating area in each damps and reinforces different harmonics, thus changing the sound.

The soft palate (velum) works as a trap door at the back of the oral cavity (see Figure 6). It opens and closes to allow access to the nasal cavity. During respiration, the soft palate is relaxed in a downward position, which allows air to enter the pharynx from the nose. When we speak, however, the soft palate tenses and moves up and back to close off the nasal cavity (except for the three American nasal consonant sounds, /m/, /n/, and /ŋ/ (as in sing)).

To feel the soft palate working, breathe in through your nose and out through your mouth. To watch this process, hold a mirror in front of your face and open your mouth wide as you breathe. You may see the uvula, the bulb-like extension of the soft palate, pulling up into the velum as it rises. The uvula adds little to our speech or to the action of the velum, but it does help demonstrate the action of the soft palate.

The soft palate is relatively slow-moving for a speech organ. Because it must close the nasal cavity to prevent nasality on inappropriate sounds, its slow action can create difficulties.

Common Resonance Problems

Nasality

With the exception of thin voices, nasality is the most common resonance problem I hear from broadcasters. The problem occurs in various ways. Some clients have **generalized nasality,** which means all their sounds go through the nasal cavity, and a true nasal voice results. Others have **assimilated nasality,** which occurs only on vowels that precede or follow /m/, /n/, or /ŋ/. This is caused by the slow-moving nature of the soft palate. In a word like "man," for example, the soft palate remains down for the vowel sound instead of rising to close off the nose for the vowel, and then relaxing again for the /n/. Still other clients have nasality or palatal placement of certain vowels, like the midwestern and New York tendency to become nasal on the vowel sounds /ɑ/ (as in "park") and /æ/ (as in "back").

There are some anatomical reasons for nasality. A cleft palate leaves a hole in the hard palate, which allows sounds to enter the nasal cavity. This is generally corrected at birth now, but in the past, cleft palate sufferers had generalized nasality all their lives. Another problem occurs when the soft palate is too short. Also, some neurological diseases, like myasthenia gravis, affect the use of muscles and, therefore, weaken the muscles of the soft palate, limiting its ability to contract and rise to close off the nasal cavity.

In most cases, however, nasality is either a learned behavior or the result of a lazy soft palate. Learned nasality may come from living in an area where nasality pervades pronunciation patterns, or copying a parent or teacher with this sound. The soft palate may lack the needed tension to close the nasal cavity. It may also result from the mouth not being opened widely enough, which can force sound into the nasal cavity.

Unfortunately, nasality is one of the hardest resonance problems to correct. Opening the mouth more will usually help. It is also beneficial to work on placement (see Resonance Warm-Ups). I have had clients who profited from lowering their pitch, but this should only be attempted with the help of a trained speech professional.

Denasality

Many people mistakenly refer to a denasal voice as nasal. Actually, denasality is the reverse of nasality. A denasal voice sounds less nasal and is often associated with a head cold. A person might say, "I have a cold id by dose," when they are speaking with a denasal voice. For this vocal production, the nasal consonants /m/, /n/, and /ŋ/ are prevented from entering the nasal cavity. This eliminates the degree of nasality that is expected in American speech.

Denasality is usually a structural problem that requires medical attention. It results from nasopharyngeal blockage that prevents sound from entering the nose. This might be a deviated septum or a growth in the nasal cavity. Allergies can also cause blockage in the nose due to swelling and secretions. And, of course, all of us occasionally suffer from head colds that change our voices. Colds will go away, but any of the other conditions should be checked by an ear, nose, and throat specialist. Removing the blockage and perhaps follow-up speech therapy will generally eliminate the denasality.

If denasality is not caused from blockage, it may be a learned behavior. Exercises to feel the soft palate movement will aid in correcting the problem (see Focus on Resonance).

Thin Voice

The most common resonance problem I encounter in broadcasters is a thin voice. This is also referred to as an immature or childish voice. In women this is often referred to as a "little girl's voice," and in men it can result in an effeminate voice. In broadcasters, a thin voice lacks an authoritative sound. It is difficult to sound credible when you have a child-like voice. In addition, when the volume is raised, this voice usually becomes shrill and strident.

Bunching the tongue up in the mouth reduces the size of the resonating cavity. When the size of a cavity is reduced, the long sound waves are more likely to be damped. If you fill a vase with water, you will hear this phenomenon. The pitch of the sound coming from the water will get higher and higher as the water fills more and more of the resonating air chamber. Most of us know when to turn off the water by the sound we hear from the vase.

If you use your tongue to restrict the size of your oral cavity, you will limit the number of long sound waves that can escape from your mouth. Your pitch will sound higher, and your voice will sound thin. You may be speaking in your optimum pitch range, but your small oral resonating cavity is killing the lower-pitched harmonics and emphasizing the ones closest to its natural resonant frequency. Because the cavity is small, its natural resonating frequency is high. What we hear is a thin, high-pitched sound.

Building a rich voice requires opening your mouth more. This does not mean you will have exaggerated lip movements for speech. Your lips may not have to open any more than they already do. What needs to be accomplished for good oral resonance is a wider opening in the back of the oral cavity. Arthur Lessac refers to this as the "inverted megaphone" approach (see Suggested Reading). If you put a small megaphone next to your cheeks, the small end would be at your lips and the wide end by your molars.

Learning to open the mouth wider in the back requires practice. Remember that the muscles that close the mouth are some of the strongest in our bodies. Dropping and relaxing the jaw means letting go of tension in the jaw area (see Warm-Ups and Focus on Resonance). A reduction of tension in this area can be accomplished, however, and the increase in resonance can be dramatic.

If you are told your pitch is too high for broadcasting, the first thing you should pursue is work on resonance. You may be using your optimum pitch, but you are sending it out through a flute instead of a tuba. Spend time doing the Resonance Warm-Ups before considering artificially lowering your pitch, which can result in problems with your vocal mechanism (and remember, pitch work should always be done with the help of a trained speech professional). You may find, as many of my clients have, that increasing your resonance gives you the sound you desire. Lowering the tongue, eliminating tension in the oral cavity, and opening the mouth and throat more are all necessary steps toward better resonance.

Placement

Another aspect of resonance is placement. Placement involves where you channel the sound waves as they come up the pharynx. If the sound waves are sent straight up the pharynx, they are likely to go into the nasal or palatal area (see Figure 6). Since these areas limit good resonance, they should not be your area of placement.

To send your sound waves into the best location for good oral resonance, you should place the sound just behind your lower front teeth. This requires bringing the sound waves up the pharynx and making a 130 degree turn into the oral cavity. It also involves sensing the vibrations extending all the way to the front teeth. Breath is a key here, since it is the energy for speech. Be certain that you are using proper breathing as described in Chapter 1.

I ask clients to visualize their placement in some manner. Some view the sound waves as a garden hose coming up from their lungs and spraying out their mouths. Others see a beam of colored light projecting from their lungs, turning to enter the oral cavity, and extending forward to their front teeth and out their mouth. I even had one radio sports announcer who envisioned his placement as a basketball being thrown in an arch.

Projection

Placing the sound correctly in the oral cavity helps create good resonance, but this needs to be followed by proper forward projection of the sound. Projection is what allows an actor or singer to be heard in the last row of a theatre without a microphone. It does not involve increasing volume but moving the sound waves forward from the mouth with intensity. Many speakers have good resonance, but they hold the sound close to their mouths and never project it well. That beam of light or stream of water you imagine needs to project through the lower front teeth and out into the air (see Resonance Warm-ups).

Good resonance should be the goal of all broadcasters. Letting our natural resonators, the pharynx, nose, and mouth, do their optimum work produces the best voice with the least amount of strain.

Focus on Resonance

To improve the resonance of your voice, you must first learn to feel the involvement of your resonators in your speech production.

A) Use a mirror to watch the movement of the soft palate. Inhale through your nose and exhale through your mouth. Watch the uvula (the bulb-like extension of the soft palate) move up and down. It moves up when the soft palate rises, closing like a trap door to block the nasal cavity as you exhale out of your mouth. When you inhale, the back of the tongue moves up to meet the soft palate as it relaxes in its downward position.

B) Now watch the movement of your soft palate and tongue as you make the following sounds:

- gah, gah, gah, gah
- ng, ng, ng, ng (as in "sing")
- ah, ah, ah, ah (as in "father")
- ah, ng, ah, ng

C) The tightest closure of the soft palate occurs for the consonant plosive sounds of /p/ /b/ and /t/ /d/. These sounds are called plosives because the air must be stopped in our mouths and pressure must build up before the air is allowed to explode out. Feel the soft palate's tight closure by making these sounds. Exaggerate the build-up of air before letting it explode out. Now begin the formation of the /p/ sound and build up extra pressure. Instead of letting it explode, release the pressure through your nose. You should feel the soft palate relaxing to let the air out the nose. You may even feel some popping in your ears.

D) To check for denasality, breathe through each nostril alone when your nasal cavity is clear. If one nostril restricts your air intake, you will feel it. Watch in a mirror as you do this. One nostril may seem to collapse when you inhale through it. You may see this at the nostril or higher up behind the bridge of the nose. Closure is a sign that there is some blockage in that nostril. You might want to have this checked by a physician. To hear the effect of denasality, hold your nostrils closed and say this phrase:

```
Now our morning money market
summary.
```

With denasality, it probably sounded like

```
Dow our bordig bodey barket subary.
```

This illustrates the important role our nasal consonants play in giving our language its distinctive sound.

E) To check for nasality, hold your nose closed and repeat the following sentences:

> Authorities agree that the gas
> could have caused the fire.
>
> The reporter will follow the
> story at six o'clock.

These sentences have no nasal sounds in them. When you hold your nose closed and say them, you should not feel any pressure in the nasal area. If you do, you have nasality to some degree. The pressure comes because you are allowing some sound to enter the nasal cavity. You feel it trying to escape from your closed nose.

F) To feel nasal resonance at work, try making the three nasal sounds. Make a strong /m/ sound by closing your lips and forcing the air into the nasal cavity. Put your index finger and thumb on the bridge of your nose and feel the vibrations as you make the sound. Now make an /n/ sound by putting the tip of your tongue against the alveolar ridge (the ridge behind the upper front teeth) and blocking the air. Again, feel the vibrations. Now make an /ŋ/ sound as in "sing." Bring your tongue up to your velum, and feel the vibrations. Next alternate between "ah" and /m/, and feel the change in vibrations. You should feel the nose vibrating for the /m/, but no vibrations with "ah."

G) To get a sense of your pharynx moving, induce a comfortable, relaxed yawn. This opens the pharynx for the maximum intake of air. Use this as a natural relaxer for the throat.

H) To illustrate how smiling affects your voice, say the vowel "ah" with the lips pulled back. Now say the vowel without a smile by dropping the jaw straight down. Listen to the difference in the quality of the sound. The first one should sound thinner and more tense than the second. You may think the pitch is different, but you should try to keep it the same. The change in the quality of the sound can be quite apparent, and it can result from the change in resonance only.

I) Our vowels are formed by changing the shape of our oral cavity, which alters the resonance. Say these vowels, gliding from one to another, and feel the oral cavity adjusting for each vowel:

- "ah"—"ee"—"awe"—"oo" (as in food).

Resonance Warm-Ups

When doing the resonance Warm-Ups, especially the ones that call for opening the back of the mouth more, you should use some caution. Do not force the jaw open too widely. This is of utmost importance if you have TMJ syndrome (temporomandibular joint dysfunction) or have had dislocations of your jaw. Symptoms of these would be pain when chewing or talking, tightness in the jaw, and clicking sounds with jaw movement. If you have any of these symptoms, open only as wide as you can without straining when you do these Warm-Ups, and consult a dental specialist to relieve the jaw problem.

1) To improve placement and increase oral resonance, bend forward from the waist at a ninety degree angle. Keep your neck straight so you are looking down at the floor. Flex your knees slightly to prevent strain on your back. (If you have a bad back, do this Warm-Up on all fours with your back straight and your face parallel to the floor.) Repeat this phrase, aiming the sound at the floor as you look down:

- Good evening, this is (your name) reporting for Eyewitness News.

Feel the sound resonating in your oral cavity before the sound falls toward the floor. Concentrate on hitting the floor with the sound. Now straighten up and repeat the phrase, keeping the placement the same.

2) The sound "ah" opens the mouth the widest and lowers the tongue. Doctors use this to look at our throats, and you can use it to increase resonance. Say the following words, preceded by "ah," and try to maintain the wide opening:

ah	far
ah	father
ah	got
ah	factor
ah	back
ah	tackle
ah	awesome
ah	awful
ah	law
ah	go
ah	own
ah	gold

3) The word "awe" puts your lips and cheeks in a position to have the best oral resonance. This position is the reverse of a smile, which pulls the lips back and tenses the cheeks. Say the word "awe" before each number as you count from one to ten to feel the relaxed, forward position of the cheeks and lips.

• Awe—1, awe—2, awe—3, etc.

4) To increase the opening in the back of the mouth, make a fist with your hand and extend the index and middle finger slightly.

With these fingers still in a bent position, place the knuckles against your cheek with your thumb toward the ground (see photograph below). The desired effect is to use the knuckles of your two bent fingers to measure an opening of an inch or more between your molars. Press these fingers against your cheek and open your mouth enough to push your knuckles between your molars. This creates a wide opening in the back of the mouth. With your fingers in this position, say these words (they may sound distorted):

- go, go, go, go
- awe, awe, awe, awe
- ah, ah, ah, ah
- at, at, at, at
- all, all, all, all
- yard, yard, yard, yard

Use the knuckles of your index and middle fingers to measure an opening between your molars.

Courtesy of WVIR–TV, Charlottesville, VA

5) Preserving the feeling of the last Warm-Up, leave your bent fingers against your cheeks. This time let them be a gauge of the size of the opening sustained while speaking. You will feel your teeth come together for some sounds, but try to maintain the wide opening when possible. Repeat these sentences, working to open the back of the mouth:

```
Good afternoon. This is
Newsbreak, and I'm (your name).

Fighting broke out again today
between rival forces.

Winter promises to bring
bitter cold to the Washington
area.

A victory today for abortion
rights supporters.
```

6) To increase jaw openness for better resonance, place your chin between your thumb and index finger. Repeat these words, feeling the jaw drop as much as possible:

- back, back, back, back
- sack, sack, sack, sack
- bad, bad, bad, bad
- yard, yard, yard, yard
- am, am, am, am
- accent, accent, accent, accent
- sang, sang, sang, sang

7) To avoid assimilated nasality, you must learn to keep vowels that precede or follow nasal sounds from having nasal production. This requires extra work to close the nasal cavity for these vowel sounds. Practice with these comparisons. The first column should be resonated in the oral cavity. Check your production of this by holding your nose closed while you say a word in the first column. You should be able to say all the words in the first column with no air pressure against your closed nose. Next say the

corresponding word in the second column, but maintain the oral resonance for the first part of the word. You can hold your nose closed until you get to the nasal sound at the end of the word to monitor your oral placement.

be	beam
tee	team
see	seam
we	wing
law	long
pay	pain
owe	own
burr	burn

In the next two columns, say the nasal sound in the first column, but in the second column, switch to oral resonance for the rest of the word after the nasal.

m	me
m	mud
m	mow
m	mitt
n	no
n	near
n	new
n	need

8) It is important to continue to work on placement of the sound waves behind the lower front teeth. Decide what imagery you want to use to see the sound beginning at the diaphragm and moving up from the lungs through the vocal folds and into the pharynx. Watch the sound waves making the important 130 degree turn to enter the oral cavity, and see the sound waves hitting the back of the lower front teeth before leaving the mouth. You might think of a beam of light, a hose, a tube, or anything that helps you visualize this path. Now repeat these vowel sounds with your eyes closed and your concentration on the sound waves making their journey:

- ah, awe, eee

- ah, awe, eee

- ah, awe, eee

Next say this sentence with the same concentration:

- My voice begins at the diaphragm, is pushed from the lungs, passes through the vocal folds into the pharynx, and turns to resonate in my oral cavity.

Keep working with this phrase until you can say it with one exhalation and imagine it moving through the vocal mechanism.

9) An important part of good resonance is projection. Using an extended "ah" sound, begin by imagining the sound coming out of your mouth through your lower front teeth. Next hold your hand about twelve inches in front of your face. Project the "ah" sound and imagine it hitting your hand. Now take your hand away and try to hit a wall several feet away with the sound. Finally, project the sound so that it goes through the wall.

This exercise should not involve an increase in volume. Think of the intensity of the sound and not the volume. If you allow the sound to originate in your abdominal area, you should get a feeling of the sound projecting forward.

Another way to think of this is to imagine how it feels to give a command to an active two-year-old child or a misbehaving puppy. You do not have to scream, which would involve an increase in volume, but you do have to be forceful. Try saying, "Sit down," with forcefulness and intensity. This should give you a feeling of proper projection of the sound.

Being conversational does not mean being sloppy or regionalistic. It takes constant work and study to make the audience listen to what is said, not who is saying it. The job of a communicator is to make it sound easy to do, even though it isn't.

Bob Bartlett
News Director, KTAB–TV
Abilene, Texas

Adopt Standard American diction. Regional identification is good only if a talent wants to remain in a specific area an entire career.

Jack Frost
News Director, KALB–TV
Alexandria, Louisiana

Many broadcasters I have worked with want to overarticulate because they think it "sounds right." Fact is, it sounds unnatural and uncomfortable.

Lee Hall
News Director, KOMO/KVI/KPLZ
Seattle, Washington

Articulation— Forming and Shaping the Sound

A healthy, well-resonated sound is worthless to you as a broadcaster and a communicator if you cannot articulate the sound into words. Words in our language are made up of phonemes (individual sounds) that combine to give meaning. We use our articulators to shape sound waves into phonemes.

Proper articulation is of utmost importance to you as a broadcaster because your voice must be carried through many different electronic devices (see Figure 7). You speak into a microphone which transfers the sound to an amplifier which is connected to a transmitter. After the sound is transmitted either by wires or satellite, it must go through a receiver and be broadcast through a speaker before it can enter the listener's ear. Every step in this process can diminish the sound. What might be heard perfectly well in face-to-face conversation may be washed out by the time it reaches the listener in electronic media. Careful articulation is imperative.

Figure 7
Electronic Communication

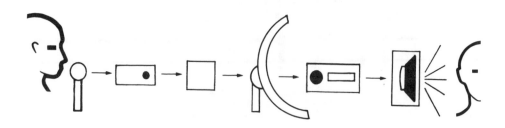

Microphone Amplifier Transmitter Satellite Receiver Speaker

Articulation Anatomy

To shape sound, we use our lips, teeth, tongue, jaw, and hard and soft palate (see Figure 8). These structures are called our articulators. We move our articulators in many ways to speak, and they are most active for consonants.

To feel the articulation of a series of consonants, first make a /p/ sound. The lips come together to stop the air and let it explode out to make the /p/. Now try a "th" sound. Begin to say the word "thin" and feel the friction that results from forcing air through the opening between the front teeth and the tongue. Now make a /t/ sound and feel the tongue tip coming in contact with the alveolar ridge. The soft palate helps with the production of /k/ and /g/ sounds. The tongue comes up to contact the soft palate. Begin to say the word "kick" and feel this movement.

Vowel sounds are made by changing the shape of the oral cavity, thereby changing the resonance. Compare the "ee" sound with "ah." The "ee" sound is produced with a limited mouth opening and a tense, high tongue. For "ah" the jaw and tongue drop

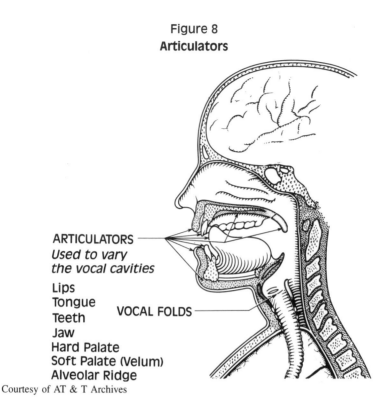

Figure 8
Articulators

ARTICULATORS
*Used to vary
the vocal cavities*

Lips
Tongue
Teeth   VOCAL FOLDS
Jaw
Hard Palate
Soft Palate (Velum)
Alveolar Ridge

Courtesy of AT & T Archives

to increase the size of the resonating cavity. All vowels depend on the tension of the mouth, the height of the tongue, and the shape of the lips for their production.

Flexibility

The expressions "lazy tongue" or "lazy mouth" indicate the importance of flexibility for good articulation. If the articulators are sluggish, it is difficult to articulate sounds clearly. Frequently this is referred to as "sloppy speech." Sometimes this is adequate in relaxed conversation, but poor articulation is never acceptable for broadcast voice.

The agility of our articulators is very important for good speech. Consider, for example, what your tongue alone has to do to say a simple sentence like, "Let Ted label that truck." Say the sentence slowly and feel the tongue moving from the alveolar ridge to the front teeth and up to the soft palate (see Figure 8). The tongue must make all this movement to produce only five words. At this rate, the tongue will make as many as 300 or more movements a minute to produce speech.

Tongue positions are only one part of the complicated combination of articulation movements required for speech. While the tongue is moving, the jaw must vary the size of the oral cavity and the soft palate must open and close the passage to the nasal cavity. All of this must be done rapidly to create the series of phonemes that make up speech. Watching an X-ray of the speech process is like seeing a finely tuned machine in motion, making hundreds of adjustments every minute.

The jaw is of utmost importance in the process of articulation. Even the most flexible tongue cannot move freely if the jaw is constricting the oral cavity. Clenched teeth not only affect resonance (see Chapter 3), but they limit the movement of the other articulators as well. Developing an open, relaxed mouth is important for both resonance and articulation (see Resonance and Articulation Warm-ups in this chapter and Chapter 3).

The articulators depend on lubrication to work properly, just like the vocal folds. Unlike the rest of the vocal tract, however, which produces mucous for lubrication, the oral cavity produces saliva. Glands under the tongue and in the back of the mouth secrete saliva. Dehydration causes a reduction in saliva, which makes articulation more difficult (see Chapter 2). Tension also may reduce the production of saliva. Public speakers are provided with a glass of water for this reason. Taking a few sips of water lubricates the mouth and relaxes the throat. You can also activate the salivary glands by sucking as if you had a mint in your mouth. You will feel the saliva coming out from under the tongue as you pretend you are sucking a mint.

Tension can also cause too much saliva to be produced. A radio client of mine called one day to ask my advice about excessive saliva. She said she had to swallow throughout her newscast because her mouth was flooded with saliva. I imagined her using a towel to wipe her mouth as the saliva poured out, but she assured me it was not quite that severe. She was worried, however, that her new job would be in jeopardy because of the problem. Using breathing exercises to relax, she overcame her tension about her new job. When the tension disappeared, so did the excess saliva.

The Sounds of Our Language

In order to articulate properly, you must know the sounds we use in our language and how to form them correctly. There are forty sounds (phonemes) required for General American speech. General American is the dialect most accepted for broadcasters.

Because we have an alphabet that uses twenty-six letters to represent forty sounds, our spelling is confusing. We cannot depend on written words for pronunciation guides. In order to know how to pronounce words, we have to depend on a more accurate system than our alphabet and spelling. We must use a sound-based method as a guide to pronunciation.

A **phoneme** is the smallest segment of sound we can produce that signals meaning. (Phonemes are printed in slash marks to distinguish the symbol for the sound from a letter in our alphabet.) If you omit the /t/ sound from the word "last," for example, you have the word "lass." Therefore, /t/ is a phoneme in the word "last." "Last" contains four phonemes: /l/, the vowel sound /æ/, /s/, and /t/. "Lass" has only three phonemes: /l/, /æ/, and /s/. Likewise, if you omit the /r/ from "crash," you have the word "cash." Phonemes signal meaning in our words.

Phonemes and spelling are not always the same, which makes our language difficult to learn to pronounce. Look at the word "thaw." It is spelled with four letters, but there are only two phonemes in the word: the /θ/ ("th" sound) and the vowel sound "aw" /ɔ/. "Bought" has six letters and only three sounds: /b/, the vowel /ɔ/, and /t/. We also have the spelling problem of silent letters like the extra "s" in the word "lass" /læs/.

Another problem with our spelling that creates pronunciation difficulty is that many of our sounds are spelled with the same letter. The letter, "e," for example, can be pronounced in six different ways: /ɑ/ as in "sergeant," /e/ as in "Jose," /i/ as in "be," /ɪ/ as in "pretty," /ɛ/ as in "pen," and /ə/ as in "item." Consider the different pronunciations of the vowel sounds represented by "ou" in the following words: through, though, thought, rough, could, loud.

There is also the problem of the same sound having different spellings. For example, the /i/ ("ee" sound) can be spelled in at least ten different ways, including "Caesar," "see," "eve" and "please." A frequently used example of this is said to have been given by George Bernard Shaw. He wrote the word "ghoti," and asked for it to be pronounced. When he reported it was the word "fish" he explained that the "gh" was as in "rough," the "o" was as in "women," and the "ti" was as in "nation."

Finding Proper Pronunciations

Knowing the proper pronunciations of words is a requirement for a good broadcaster. The *United Press International Broadcast Stylebook* says that it is as important for a broadcaster to know how to pronounce words correctly as it is for a newspaper writer to know how to spell them. As broadcasters, you have an obligation to the public to set a standard for correct pronunciation.

In the past, networks have often provided help with establishing standard pronunciations. Dr. Cabell Greet, a former professor at Barnard College, was a pronunciation and grammar consultant for CBS for nearly fifteen years. He carefully screened broadcasts and sent memos to reporters when corrections were needed. Today, broadcasters usually are responsible for polishing their own pronunciations.

There are three places you can look when you need to find the proper pronunciation of a word:

1. the dictionary,

2. the wire service,

3. a phonetic dictionary.

The Dictionary

You are probably familiar with the use of a dictionary for pronunciation. Dictionaries use a system called diacritical markings to show pronunciations of each word they list. These markings can be helpful, but they are sometimes hard to decipher because they vary from publisher to publisher. Also, they depend on unfamiliar markings like macrons (a line above a letter), umlauts (two dots above a letter), and breves (a curved line above a letter).

If you are marking your script to help you remember the pronunciation of a particular word, diacritical markings do not always work well. The markings above letters can be difficult to see, and the system may be hard to remember.

The Wire Service

The wire services offer daily pronunciation guides for difficult words and names (see Figure 9). Phonetic spellings or "pronouncers" are given, using the letters of our alphabet. Here is the key to the AP broadcast pronunciation style, provided by Associated Press Broadcast Services:

Vowel Sounds:

```
  a -- apple, bat          oh -- go, oval
 ah -- father, hot         oo -- food, two
 aw -- law, long           ow -- how, now
 ay -- ace, fate           oy -- boy
  e -- bed                  u -- foot, put
ehr -- merry              uh -- puff
 ee -- see, tea            ur -- burden, curl
  i -- pin, middle   y, eye -- ice, time
```

Consonants:

```
  g -- got, beg           sh -- shut
  j -- jem, job            z -- zoom
  k -- cap, keep          zh -- mirage
 ch -- chair              kh -- gutteral ''k''
  s -- see
```

Figure 9
AP Daily Pronunciation Guide

```
News <
Aqaba -- AH'-kah-bah
Jean-Bertrand Aristide -- zhahn behr-TRAHN'
  ahr-ihs-TEED'
Hafez Assad -- HAH'-fez AH'-sahd
Bosnia-Herzegovina -- BAHZ'-nee-ah
  hurt-suh-goh-VEE'-nah
Boutros Boutros-Ghali -- BOO'-trohs BOO'-trohs
  KHAL'-ee
John Breaux -- broh
Burundi -- boo-ROON'-dee
Raoul Cedras -- rah-OOL' SAY'-drahs
Benjamin Chavis -- CHAY'-vihs
Lake Chelan -- shuh-LAN'
Frank Chiuchiolo -- chyoo-chee-OH'-loh
E. coli -- ee KOH'-ly
Deshutes National Forest -- duh-SHOOTS'
Duchesne -- doo-SHAYN'
Eilat -- AY'-laht
Entiat -- EHN'-tee-aht
Lauch Faircloth -- lahk
Ejup Ganich -- AY'-oop GAH'-nich
Gorazde -- goh-RAHZH'-deh
Hezbollah -- hez-boh-LAH'
King Hussein -- hoo-SAYN'
Hutu -- HOO'-too
Harold Ickes -- IH'-keez
Lance Ito -- EE'-toh
Emile Jonassaint -- joh-nah-SAHN'
Kim Jong Il -- kim jahng ihl
George Joulwan -- JOWL'-wahn
Kamannyola -- kah-mah-NYOH'-lah
Radovan Karadzic -- RA'-doh-van KA'-ra-dich
Kigali -- kee-GAH'-lee
Robert Malval -- roh-BEHR' mahl-VAHL'
Kweisi Mfume -- kwah-EE'-see oom-FOO'-may
Slobodan Milosevic -- SLOH'-boh-dahn
  mee-LOHSH'-uh-vich
```

Pale -- PAH'-leh
Federico Pena -- PAYN'-yuh
Shimon Peres -- shee-MOHN' PEHR'-ehs
Qazvin -- kahz-VEEN'
Yitzhak Rabin -- YIT'-sahk rah-BEEN'
Donald Re -- ray
Robert Reich -- rysh
Donald Riegle -- REE'-guhl
Rwanda -- ruh-WAHN'-dah
Muhamed Sacirbey -- SHAHK'-ur-bay
San Cristobal de las Casas -- sahn
  CREE'-stoh-bahl day lahs KAH'-sahs
Sarajevo -- sehr-uh-YAY'-voh
Saugerties -- SAW'-gur-teez
Nabil Shaath -- nah-BEEL' shahth
Donna Shalala -- shuh-LAY'-luh
John Shalikashvili -- shah-lee-kash-VEE'-lee
Haris Silajdzic -- sih-LY'-jihch
Srpska -- SEHRB'-skuh
George Stephanopoulos -- stef-uh-NAH'-puh-luhs
Tyee Creek -- ty-EE'
Tutsi -- TOOT'-see
Verdi, Nevada -- VUR'-dy
Wedowee -- weh-DOW'-wee
Ezer Weizman -- AY'-zur WYTZ'-mahn
Zaire -- zah-EER'

  Sports <
Paul Azinger -- AY'-zing-ur
Surya Bonaly -- SUR'-yah BOH'-nah-lee
Gene Budig -- BYOO'-dihg
Colin Campbell -- KOH'-lihn
Tony Casillas -- kah-SEE'-uhs
Donald Fehr -- feer
Kent Hrbek -- HUR'-behk
Jaromir Jaqr -- YAHR'-oh-mihr YAH'-gur
Richard Krajicek -- KRY'-ih-chehk
Toni Kukoc -- KOO'-kohch
Mario Lemieux -- leh-MYOO'
Corey Pavin -- PAY'-vihn
Paul Tagliabue -- TAG'-lee-uh-boo

This system is helpful, but it is limited because it is based on the letters of our alphabet. It is impossible to give a phonetic transcription of every word in our language using only the alphabet. The wire services often resort to rhyming to make their pronunciations clear. UPI, for example, compares the name "Roger Blough," to the pronunciation of "now."

The main advantage of the wire service pronunciation guides is that they deal with proper names and places that are in the current news. It is advisable to save the daily pronunciation guides given by the wire services. You might want to develop your own file or notebook of these guides. This will help you pronounce the many foreign names and places that are in the news every day.

It is also a good idea to add local pronunciations to your personal guide. When you first move to a station, ask other reporters about local pronunciations. "Cairo" in Illinois, for example, is pronounced "Kayro." In Maryland, "Grosvenor" is pronounced "Grovner," and in Missouri, "New Madrid" does not sound the same as "Madrid, Spain." The emphasis is on the first syllable in the Missouri pronunciation. Your credibility with your local audience will be ruined if you mispronounce local names.

A Phonetic Dictionary

The International Phonetic Alphabet (IPA) contains hundreds of symbols to transcribe all languages. Forty of these symbols represent the most frequently used sounds in American speech. This alphabet relies on most of the twenty-six letters of our alphabet and adds ten symbols to cover all forty sounds. (The letters C, Q, Y, and X are omitted because they are represented by the sounds /k/ or /s/, /kju/, /j/, and /ɛks/.) The IPA was developed because a group of scholars attending an international convention of language teachers in 1888 were aware of the difficulty of transcribing English without a phonetic alphabet. It has been used since that time as the most accurate guide to pronunciation.

A phonetic symbol represents only one sound and does not change its pronunciation. The symbol /i/, for example, always represents the sound "ee" as in bee. When you see a word written in phonetics that includes an /i/, you can be confident that sound is "ee." The word "bee" would be written /bi/ in phonetics. Knowing this symbol, you can easily pronounce these words written in phonetics: /ti/, /ki/, /mit/, /lin/ (tea, key, meet, lean).

The advantages of using the IPA are that it is easy to learn and remember, it is easy to write on your copy, and it is the only accepted international set of symbols used for pronunciation. You will find that most speech and linguistics books use the IPA. It is also used by many foreign-language dictionaries, such as those by Cassell. Because the IPA uses most of the letters of our alphabet, it is not difficult to remember. Words you write in phonetics in your copy are easy to see and pronounce.

As a broadcaster, it is well worth the effort to commit the symbols to memory and begin using them. Once you have mastered the symbols, you will have a tool you can use the rest of your career.

Several dictionaries use phonetics for their pronunciation guide, such as *The NBC Handbook of Pronunciation* (Harper & Row) which adapts the IPA and has been a standard reference book for broadcasters for many years. Another source is *NTC's Dictionary of American English Pronunciation* (see Suggested Readings).

Kenyon and Knott's *A Pronouncing Dictionary of American English* (Merriam-Webster) is considered the bible of pronunciation by most speech and linguist professionals. It is also an excellent pronunciation reference guide for broadcasters. There is a key to the IPA in the front of this dictionary, which makes it a handy reference guide whether you know the IPA or not.

Kenyon and Knott's dictionary lists only the pronunciations of words. The pronunciations are given in all three of the accepted dialects in this country: General American, Eastern, and Southern. (A word like "fare," for example, is listed as /fɛr/ for General American, /fɛə/ without the /r/ for Eastern, and /fæə/ without the /r/ and using the vowel as in "at" for Southern.) The only shortcoming of this dictionary is that it was published in 1953. Pronunciations change fairly slowly in this country, but it is a good idea to check any confusing pronunciations in a more current dictionary (see Selected References in Chapter 6).

The IPA for Broadcasters

The IPA is divided into consonants and vowels just like our alphabet (see Figure 10). These categories are then classified by the method of production.

Figure 10
The Complete International Phonetic Alphabet for American English
(See Appendix C for more practice words and a comparison of AP, IPA, & dictionary symbols.)

VOICED

Vowels

/i/	bee
/ɪ/	bit
/e/	say
/ɛ/	bet
/æ/	at
/ɑ/	spa
/ɔ/	caw
/o/	oak
/u/	two
/ʊ/	put
/ə/	above
/ɚ/	father

Diphthongs

/ju/	use
/aɪ/	eye
/aʊ/	cow
/ɔɪ/	toy

Consonants

VOICELESS		VOICED	
/t/	to	/d/	do
/p/	pop	/b/	boy
/k/	key	/g/	got
/f/	fit	/v/	van
/θ/	thin	/ð/	them
/s/	say	/z/	zip
/ʃ/	she	/ʒ/	casual
/h/	hit		
/tʃ/	chip	/dʒ/	Jim
		/w/	was
		/j/	yet
		/r/	run
		/l/	love
		/m/	miss
		/n/	now
		/ŋ/	sing

Vowels

Vowels in our language are all voiced, meaning that the vocal folds vibrate for their production. Vowels are formed by changes in resonance and are classified as pure vowels or diphthongs. Pure vowels can be extended indefinitely when produced. You can say /i/ ("ee"), for example, until you run out of air. Diphthongs, on the other hand, change articulation during pronunciation. They require movement of the mouth for their production, since they are composed of two vowel sounds coming together. Say the vowel in "toy," and you will feel your mouth moving for its production.

Our usual a-e-i-o-u symbols are inadequate when it comes to representing the sixteen vowel sounds in our language. The IPA uses these symbols for the vowel phonemes (see Appendix C for more practice words):

	Pure Vowels		**Diphthongs**
/i/	bee	/ju/	use
/ɪ/	bit	/aɪ/	eye
/e/	say	/aʊ/	cow
/ɛ/	bet	/ɔɪ/	toy
/æ/	at		
/ɑ/	spa		
/ɔ/	caw		
/o/	oak		
/u/	two		
/ʊ/	put		
/ə/	above		
/ɚ/	father		

Consonants

To produce consonants in English we either stop or partially stop the air as it comes from the mouth. Consonants are, therefore, classified by the method of releasing the air, the position of the articulators when they are produced, and whether they are voiced or not.

Voicing is perhaps the easiest distinguishing factor of consonants. To understand the difference in voicing, put your fingers on your larynx and begin to say the word "to." Stop after you have made the /t/ sound and repeat the /t/ several times. Next make a /d/ sound as in the word "do." You should feel vibrations in your larynx for the /d/ and none for the /t/. These particular consonants are called cognates because they are articulated in the same manner, but one sound is voiced and one is voiceless. There are eight cognate pairs in our language:

	Voiceless		**Voiced**
/t/	to	/d/	do
/p/	pop	/b/	boy
/k/	key	/g/	got
/f/	fit	/v/	van

/θ/	"th" thin	/ð/	them
/s/	say	/z/	zip
/ʃ/	"sh" she	/ʒ/	casual
/tʃ/	"ch" chip	/dʒ/	Jim

Using the classifying method of where the air is released and the position of the articulators, the consonants are grouped in the following manner:

-Stops or Plosives-

These sounds are formed by stopping the air and letting it explode out to produce the phoneme. For the /t/ /d/ sounds, the tongue goes to the alveolar ridge to stop the air. The /p/ /b/ are formed by the lips closing to block the air. The /k/ /g/ involve the back of the tongue coming up to the soft palate to block the air (see Figure 8).

Voiceless		**Voiced**	
/t/	to	/d/	do
/p/	pop	/b/	boy
/k/	key	/g/	got

-Fricatives-

Fricatives result from friction created by forcing air through a small opening between the articulators. These sounds can be extended until all air has been exhausted.

Voiceless		**Voiced**	
/f/	fit	/v/	van
/θ/	thin	/ð/	them
/s/	say	/z/	zip
/ʃ/	she	/ʒ/	casual
/h/	hit		

-Affricates-

These two sounds are similar to fricatives, but they include a plosive. Unlike the fricatives, their production cannot be extended because of the plosive included in each phoneme.

Voiceless	**Voiced**
/tʃ/ chip	/dʒ/ Jim

-Glides-

Glides are distinguished by the movement of the tongue during formation. They are also affected by vowel sounds and are sometimes called semivowels. The /w/ sound is the only glide that can be voiced or voiceless, but the voicing is difficult to distinguish.

Voiced

/w/   was
/j/   yet
/r/   run

-Lateral-

The /l/ sound is unique in our language. All our phonemes are produced by sending the sound straight out of the mouth or up through the nose except for the /l/ sound. This phoneme is produced by putting the tip of the tongue on the alveolar ridge (see Figure 8) and holding it there while the sides of the tongue drop. The sound is then allowed to escape from the mouth over the edges of the tongue.

Voiced

/l/   love

-Nasals-

These sounds are produced by closing off the oral cavity and allowing the sound waves to enter the nasal cavity. For the /m/ our lips come together to block the air. The /n/ sound is formed by the tongue rising to make contact with the side teeth and the alveolar ridge to block the air. For the /ŋ/ sound, the back of the tongue and the soft palate come together to block the air, forcing it to escape through the nose.

Voiced

/m/ miss
/n/ now
/ŋ/ sing

Articulation Problems

There are three basic ways in which our articulation can be faulty. We can omit necessary sounds, substitute or add sounds, or produce sounds incorrectly.

Omissions

Consonants cause the most problems involving omissions of sounds. This is unfortunate for broadcasters because consonants are so important to intelligibility and credibility. Broadcasting makes the omission problem worse because consonants often lose strength when sent through electronic media (see Figure 7).

Consonants add clarity to our language. If you say the word "oil" so that it sounds like "all," most people still know what you mean even though you are saying the vowel incorrectly. If you omit the /l/, however, you are no longer clear to your listener, even if the vowel is perfectly pronounced. Without proper consonant articulation, meaning may suffer.

One of the biggest challenges of articulation is to say your consonant phonemes correctly without sounding overpronounced. When you first begin working on pronouncing your consonants, you will most likely sound overpronounced. Only practice will eliminate the overly-precise sound.

Because consonants add clarity, it is important to form each one properly. If you say "last," for instance, and do not let the air explode out for the /t/, you have said "lass." Similarly, if you say "ass" for "ask," you have pronounced a different word. Remember that a phoneme is the smallest segment of spoken sound that signals meaning. If you leave out a phoneme, which you would be doing if you did not complete the plosive sound of the /k/ in "ask," you may be saying a different word.

The plosive consonant phonemes cause the most omission problems. The six plosive consonant phonemes are cognates:

Voiceless		**Voiced**	
/t/	to	/d/	do
/p/	pop	/b/	boy
/k/	key	/g/	got

These plosives require a burst of air for their production. If you hold your hand in front of your mouth, you should feel a puff of air as you say each of these phonemes.

The sentence, "Last winter the lists show it snowed two feet," requires the production of initial, medial, and final plosives. Say this sentence out loud. If it sounds like, "Lass winner the lis show i snow two fee," you know you have not pronounced your consonant plosive phonemes, and you have lost the intelligibility of the sentence.

I advise my clients to decide how precise they want their delivery to sound. Once they have decided if they want a relaxed, very conversational sound, or a more credible, precise delivery, they can begin to work on consonant plosives.

In the sentence, "Last winter the lists show it snowed two feet," everyone needs to pronounce the consonant plosives in the words "last," "two," and "feet" in order to achieve intelligibility. That would represent the least precise end of a continuum of articulation. For a more precise sound, you should also pronounce the consonant plosives in "winter" and "it." The most precise delivery would include correct pronunciation of the plosives in "lists" and "snowed." Pronouncing these last two words correctly requires very flexible articulators and practice to make the sentence sound natural.

Listening to broadcasters, you will hear omissions of consonant plosives to greater and lesser degrees. Remember the continuum as you listen to other broadcasters. Some will have very precise deliveries while others omit most plosives. Ed Bliss remembers Lowell Thomas saying he grew up hearing his father shout, "Articulate, son!" Thomas' delivery reflected this precision of articulation. You will notice that intelligibility, credibility, and precision of pronunciation are all linked. In Appendix A, you will see that 17 percent of news directors say they like a precise delivery. For this reason, working to pronounce ending and medial consonant plosives can be helpful (see Articulation Warm-Ups).

There are some problems, however, with consonant plosive production. One is that overpronouncing these endings can make you sound pedantic. This is especially true if you stress consonant plosives in nonessential words. Say, "The gunman ran, but the county police captured him." If you overpronounce the /t/ sounds in "but" and "county," you have taken away from the meaning of the sentence. You need to produce these /t/ sounds correctly, but you should not stress them.

You may find you are overpronouncing when you first begin to work on your consonant plosive production. The example sentence, "Last winter the lists show it snowed two feet," may require a great deal of practice to pronounce correctly. At first, you may sound like Eliza Doolittle in *My Fair Lady*, as you work to hit every plosive sound. The goal is for the production to be correct without drawing attention to the phonemes. This takes practice (see Articulation Warm-Ups).

Another problem associated with plosives is the popping sound that sometimes results from these phonemes. This is most noticeable on the /p/ and /b/ sounds. If you find popping is a problem, try speaking across the microphone instead of directly into it. You might also find lowering the microphone away from your mouth helps. Most of the time, changing the position of the microphone will eliminate the popping. If it doesn't, talk to your engineer

Lowell Thomas anchored the first regularly scheduled radio network news report in 1930, and his career continued for 45 years.

Courtesy of CBS News.

about the problem. Certain microphones are more sensitive to popping, and a change in microphones or a wind screen may be needed.

Substitutions

There are many possibilities for substitutions of one phoneme for another in our pronunciations. Foreign speakers, for example, often have substitution problems with five or ten different phonemes. A French speaker, for example, might say "sink" for "think." Broadcasters tend to have three substitutions that are most common.

1) /t/ and /d/ for /θ/ and /ð/

Working in the Washington, D.C., area, I have found the substitution of /t/ or /d/ for the "th" sounds to be a problem for many of my clients. This substitution has become part of a generalized speech pattern called "Big City Dialect." It does not matter if you are from D.C. or Los Angeles or New York City, this substitution is part of your dialect. One possible reason for this substitution localizing to big cities may be the fact that many foreign languages like French, German, and Spanish do not use the phonemes /θ/ and /ð/. Cities with large foreign populations suffer from the substitution because non-native speakers have difficulty forming the "th" sound. /t/ and /d/ are easier for them to use. If you live in a big city, you hear this substitution being made around you all the time, and you may begin to use it yourself.

This speech pattern is often associated with the stereotypical athlete who might say, "De coach put de tickets in dere." Few broadcasters would be this far off in the correct pronunciation of "th," but even a few substitutions can hurt your credibility. It is important to form these sounds correctly (see Articulation Warm-Ups).

2) /w/ for /l/

The /w/-/l/ substitution is also a frequent problem. This substitution affects pronunciations of words like, "bottle," "table," and "pull." Instead of producing the /l/ phoneme in these words, a /w/ is substituted. The words then sound like, "bottw," "tabw," and "puw." With this substitution, clarity is lost, and speech sounds childish.

3) /w/ for /r/

The /w/ phoneme is an easy one to produce, so it often substitutes for the /r/ sound in addition to the /l/. /r/ is a difficult phoneme that requires a tense, high tongue and a gliding motion of the tongue and lips. It is easier to relax the tongue and substitute a /w/ for the /r/. When this happens, a sentence like, "The rough road was dry," becomes "The wough woad was dwy." The result again is a childish, almost cartoon-character voice.

Additions

Additions also cause problems with pronunciation. Easterners, for example, may suffer from an intrusive /r/ sound. When this happens, "wash" becomes "warsh" and "America" becomes "Americur." Southerners may extend vowel sounds by adding an additional phoneme. One syllable words like "pen," "men," and "an," become two syllables with this addition.

Faulty Articulation

Incorrect production of phonemes is most often associated with a regional accent. Many factors contribute to a regional accent, including where you spent your formative speech years and where your parents are from. If you produce a flat "i" sound by failing to complete the production of the diphthong /aɪ/ in the phrase, "right nice, bright night," for example, you or your language role models may be from certain parts of the South. A nasal /æ/ sound as in "back" (produced by the tongue being too high and tense) will identify you as a Midwesterner or a New Yorker.

In casual speech, regional pronunciations are not incorrect as long as they are within our two accepted regional dialects, Eastern and Southern. As a broadcaster, however, you should adhere to General American pronunciations unless your news director advises otherwise. Many news directors prefer General American speech, as revealed by the twenty percent who indicated in the survey (Appendix A) that regional accents were a problem.

There are some stations, such as country radio stations, that occasionally want a regional sound. There are times when a station will actually train you to speak the dialect of their region. This happened to a friend from Long Island who went to a Texas station. Her first few weeks there were spent learning a Texas accent and eliminating her Long Island sound. If you find yourself in a situation like this, Kenyon and Knott's dictionary, which lists all three accepted dialects, can help you learn a regional accent.

Faulty articulation also involves lisps and excessive sibilance (hissing sound). These problems occur on fricative sounds like /s/ /z/, and /ʃ/ /ʒ/. These phonemes give speakers more trouble with production than any others.

A lisp results from improper placement of the tongue for /s/ and /z/. A frontal lisp produces a "th" sound for /s/ and /z/. Instead of "Suzy sat in the swing," a frontal lisper would say, "Thuzy that in the thwing." Pulling the tongue back will usually alleviate the problem of a frontal lisp.

A bilateral lisp is a harder problem to describe and correct. What happens in its production is that the tip of the tongue makes contact with the alveolar ridge (see Figure 8) and the /s/ or /z/ is produced by the sound going over the sides of the tongue. This is similar to the production of an /l/ phoneme. To correct this, make certain that the sides of the tongue hug the teeth, and the phoneme is produced by friction in the front of the mouth.

Whistling "s" sounds are occasionally a problem for broadcasters. This results from a narrowing of the groove in the tongue through which the air is to escape. Shortening the duration of the /s/ and /z/ phonemes will usually correct this problem.

Excessive sibilance in general can be corrected by shortening the duration of the /s/ and /z/ phonemes. If you feel your sibilant sounds distract from your delivery, try keeping their production light and short.

Focus on Articulation

A) Poor articulation results from omissions, substitutions and additions, and faulty articulation. To understand the effect of omissions, say the following word pairs and note the phoneme omitted in the second word:

center	sinner	/t/
ask	ass	/k/
winter	winner	/t/
picture	pitcher	/k/
field	feel	/d/
last	lass	/t/
painting	paining	/t/

Notice that omitting the consonant phonemes resulted in a different word being produced.

To experience the /w/-/r/ substitution, say these word pairs:

rag	wag
rate	wait
rock	wok
run	won

B) The tongue plays an important role in the production of vowel phonemes. Say these phonemes, and feel the tongue dropping progressively and the mouth opening as you move down the list (try putting your finger lightly on your tongue to feel this movement):

/i/	as in bee
/ɪ/	as in bit or /u/ as in two
/ɛ/	as in bet or /ʊ/ as in put
/æ/	as in at
/ɑ/	as in spa

C) The /t/ phoneme is usually produced with no voicing and an explosion of air, but there is one exception. In our language, it often sounds overpronounced to use a full /t/ phoneme before a syllabic /l/, /m/, or /n/. Syllabic sounds are produced when consonants form syllables without a full vowel. In these instances, the /t/ may become imploded, or it may sound more like a /d/. Some examples of syllabic sounds preceded by /t/ are:

little	bottom
rattle	button
cattle	mitten
kettle	kitten
bottle	cotton

Articulation Warm-Ups

Forming and shaping sound requires agile articulators and a good ear to monitor pronunciations. If you were training to be a ballet dancer, you would recognize the importance of exercising your body to make it flexible. Warm-ups and stretches would be part of your everyday life. You would also find you needed to practice your dance moves in front of a mirror to continue to improve. As a broadcaster, you should think of your voice in the same way. You are working with muscles, tissue, and ligaments when you are speaking. Your articulators must be as agile as a dancer's body to produce good speech. In addition, just as a dancer practices in front of a mirror, you must monitor your pronunciations to keep them correct.

Warming up our articulators before speech is imperative. Not many of us would walk out our front door and try to run a marathon without stretching our muscles. Stretching brings blood into the muscles which helps them work more effectively.

Do not be embarrassed about doing warm-up exercises. Professional singers and actors know the importance of warm-ups. As a broadcaster, your voice should be prepared prior to on-air work, just as other vocal professionals prepare. By doing warm-ups, you are showing your professionalism.

1) Say these phonemes, exaggerating the mouth positions:

- /ɑ/ as in spa

- /ɔ/as in caw

- /u/ as in two

- /i/ as in bee

Open the mouth wide for /ɑ/, round the lips for /ɔ/, pull the lips forward in a pucker for the /u/ phoneme, and smile widely for /i/. Continue to say these phonemes in an exaggerated manner, gliding from one to the next. Use this series of phonemes as a warm-up before going on air. After repeating them a dozen times or more in an exaggerated manner you should feel your mouth becoming more flexible.

2) Continuing with the exaggerated stretching from the last Warm-Up, repeat this sentence, extending the vowel phonemes:

- You see Oz.

Pucker the lips tightly for "you." Pull the lips back in a wide smile for "see," and drop the jaw and open wide for "Oz." Repeat this sentence with these exaggerated lip positions as many times as you need to in order to warm-up your articulators.

3) Repeat the following sentences as fast as you can while preserving the consonant plosive formations:

- Put a cup. Put a cup. Put a cup. Put a cup.

- Drink buttermilk. Drink buttermilk. Drink buttermilk.

Rapid repetition of these sentences will help warm-up your tongue. Say these sentences rapidly before on-air work. Be sure you feel air exploding out on the plosive sounds.

4) Chewing and talking at the same time has been used extensively to improve articulation, because chewing loosens the jaw and tongue. To practice this, pretend you have just taken a big bite from an apple and count while you chew. You can also say the months of the year, days of the week, or the alphabet for this Warm-Up. You should exaggerate your chewing while you speak.

5) Ending consonant plosives are difficult to articulate properly. Use the following word lists to practice plosive endings. Hold your hand in front of your mouth and try to feel a burst of air at the end of each word:

Ending Consonant Plosives

/t/	/d/
hit	had
mitt	lad
sit	fad
last	tried
fast	fried
past	filled
laughed	bend
craft	bird

/p/	/b/
top	bob
flop	sob
hop	lob
pipe	web
ripe	grab
deep	curb
seep	stab
leap	tab

/k/	/g/
peak	lag
sneak	hog
freak	frog
slick	log
talk	jog
make	drug
pick	snug

6) For precise broadcast speech, ending consonant plosives must also be formed correctly in sentences. This involves the same burst of air for each ending consonant plosive that you experienced when you practiced Warm-Up 5. Use the following practice sentences and news copy to improve your ending consonant plosives. Before you begin, mark each ending consonant plosive by underlining, circling, or highlighting. Tape record your reading. Exaggerate the sounds as you say them if you need to. You may sound overpronounced and technical at first. Since these are exercises, do not worry about the technical sound. Continue to practice the sentences and news copy until you can make the delivery more natural while preserving the correct production of the ending consonant plosives.

/t/ /d/
1. West Grand Junction will be hot instead of mild next week.
2. The reporter missed the fight when he jumped from the boat.
3. Word of the shot was called into the station by Rod.
4. The ride was a bad one for the East Coast bird group.
5. In the last game, just one score, Maryland eighty and Washington one hundred.

/p/ /b/
1. A gunman tried to rob the Jog Shop on Curb Street.
2. Pop culture is booming in Deep Creek.

3. Bob will keep a tab on the shop next week.
4. The mob pushed off the curb and toppled the cab.
5. The dog will jump in your lap but the cat will not.

/k/ /g/

1. The West League hit its peak in Lake Placid.
2. Smog will clog the roadways as we dig out from under the snow.
3. The dark will make a rescue effort difficult.
4. The guard will pick up the sleek car at the yard.
5. He will jog the last leg of the race in the dark.

Broadcast Copy to Practice for Ending Plosives

Gunfire shattered the quiet town of Grand Junction in Montgomery County last night. Two men were dead at the scene, another hospitalized following what police suspect was a domestic dispute.

Amtrak officials suspect a faulty rod on the rail line may have made a difficult commute for West bound passengers. Bob Bennett reported that the stop in Westchester County was the result of a break in the rail rod.

In basketball this evening, first in the NBA, it was the Atlanta Hawks over the Washington Bullets one-twenty to one-thirteen. College scores were not as close. It was

    Memphis over the University
    of Maryland ninety-eight to
    eighty-eight and Stanford beat
    Georgia Tech in a rout--ninety
    to forty-eight.

7) Consonant clusters are the most difficult consonants to pronounce. They can be learned by practicing the production of the cluster alone before attempting to incorporate it into words. Repeat clusters alone until you can say them easily and then try the words. This requires very facile articulators. Here are the most common clusters:

Voiceless		**Voiced**	
/ts/	as in bats	/dz/	as in rods
/pt/	as in wrapped	/bd/	as in robbed
/kt/	as in talked	/gd/	as in lagged
/θs/	as in fifths	/ðz/	as in breathes
/sks/	as in desks		
/sts/	as in lists		
/kθ/	as in length and strength		

8) Substitutions often involve the use of /w/ instead of /l/ or /r/. Use these word lists to practice your production of these phonemes. The /w/ is formed by pursing the lips and relaxing the tongue. The /l/ requires the tip of the tongue to make contact with the alveolar ridge or the front teeth. The sound is then allowed to escape from the mouth by dropping the sides of the tongue. The lips can be pulled back for the /l/ sound in practice to make certain they are not pursed as for /w/. Watch your production of these two phonemes in the mirror and be certain the lips are pulled back for /l/. You can force a smile by pulling the lips back for the /l/ in practice to exaggerate the production.

pull	chill
sail	mail
meal	spool
roll	fail

An /r/ requires a gliding movement of the tongue and lips. The lips are pursed at first and then they relax. The tongue is more tense for the production of /r/ than for /w/.

rock	dry
room	pretend
report	travel
dream	around

9) The /t/-/d/ substitution for /θ/ /ð/ involves the tongue being pulled too far back in the mouth. To produce a correct "th" sound, let the tongue tip come under the upper front teeth, making light contact. Friction should be produced by forcing air through the space between the front teeth and the tongue. To test your production of this, say the following words while watching your mouth in a mirror. You should be able to see your tongue each time you make the "th" phoneme. You might want to begin by lightly biting your tongue tip to position it under your teeth.

Voiceless	Voiced
thank	them
thick	the
thigh	than
thorn	they
thrill	that
think	those
ether	then
wealthy	though
nothing	seething
birthday	lather
bath	worthy
path	breathe
mouth	soothe
south	teethe
worth	loathe
faith	weather

You must use your voice as a tool for communication not as a club of attention. A well-modulated, conversational delivery is a much better form of communication than one which plumbs the heights and depths of vocal range and emotion.

James L. Walrod
Managing Editor, WEVU–TV
Bonita Springs, Florida

Follow the pointers on copy marking, and your delivery will be far more effective and expressive.

Loren Omoto
News Director, KNOW–FM
Saint Paul, Minnesota

Good anchors know their copy and relate that knowledge to the listener by using proper inflection. It also is important to realize that the job of a good anchor is not to fill every moment with the sound of their voice. A well-placed pause can be very effective.

Brian Gann
News Director, KVOO–AM/FM
Tulsa, Oklahoma

Enhancing Meaning through Stress and Intonation

There are few topics besides style of delivery that news directors so unanimously agree upon. Appendix A shows that 93 percent of those who responded to our survey marked "Conversational" as the preferred style of delivery. This is an increase from 84 percent in 1990. News directors also ranked "Monotone" as a major vocal problem. They emphasized their choice with comments like these:

"Relax and talk *to* viewers not *at* them."

"The key to good delivery is to make the broadcast sound like a conversation."

"We want natural-sounding people."

"Talk to us as if you are telling a story to a friend."

"Most listeners want people who sound real."

"Be natural."

"My best advice is simply to relax and tell a story."

Unfortunately, "relaxing and telling a story" is not the easiest thing to do. Many of my clients say that no matter how much they relax, they still sound stiff in the sound booth. It is difficult to read and not sound like you are reading.

A Broadcasting Communication Model

One of the reasons for this difficulty is that most broadcast work is an unnatural communication event. We all know how to use stress and intonation to tell a good story to a friend. Recall the last time you told a colleague about a traffic jam you encountered or an exciting event from your last vacation. Your pitch no doubt went up and down as you talked, and you may have stretched words out to build suspense. You probably got louder to emphasize words, and you may have talked faster to hold interest. In conversation, all of this comes naturally to most of us.

When we talk to someone in conversation, we participate in a communication loop (see Figure 11) that involves sending out a message and receiving feedback from the listener. The feedback we receive may be verbal, with comments like "Really?" or "I see," or it may be a nonverbal nod of the head or a puzzled look. This feedback helps us adjust our delivery to hold the interest of our listener.

Broadcasters in a sound booth, or talking to a camera, work without the help of feedback. The communication loop is truncated (see Figure 11). Messages are sent out, but no feedback exists to help the broadcaster make the subtle adjustments needed in stress and intonation to make the delivery interesting. This is why a monotone or an overdone delivery can happen in the sound booth or when talking to the camera. If you are looking at your printed copy or the wall in the sound booth, it is difficult to sound natural.

Figure 11
Communication Models

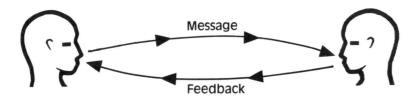

Message

Feedback

A Normal Communication Interaction

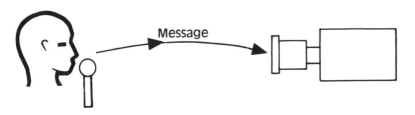

Message

A Broadcasting Interaction

Likewise, with the camera as your focal point, the communication loop is not complete.

There are two effective ways I have found to help clients sound comfortable and conversational while they stress the proper words. Both of these methods involve creating a way to superimpose a conversational delivery on a written text. A marking system can recreate a conversational style, and this system is explained in the remainder of this chapter. Another method that stresses an interpersonal communication approach is presented in Chapter 6. This involves recreating the feedback that is missing when you read a script. One or both of these methods can be used to develop a natural-sounding delivery.

Much of a reporter's on-air time is spent talking to a camera or a sound booth wall.

Courtesy of KSL–TV, Salt Lake City, UT

Developing A Broadcast Delivery Style

To compensate for the lack of natural delivery, many broadcasters develop a pattern. They realize their delivery sounds flat, so they make an arbitrary choice to stress every third word or every noun or verb. This results in a singsong delivery pattern. Fifty-five percent of the news directors responding to the survey said that one of the main delivery problems they hear is the singsong pattern.

Any predictable delivery pattern can distract from the meaning of your copy. If the audience begins to notice your delivery pattern, they have shifted their focus from content to style. Your manner of speaking should never draw more attention than the ideas you are trying to get across to your listener. In addition, a set delivery style restricts the variation that is needed for different types of stories. Within one news report, an anchor may go from a serious opening story that calls for credibility and concern to a kicker that requires a light delivery. Set delivery patterns do not allow for this kind of variety.

A client recently complained that when she does serious stories she sounds credible, but occasionally she fears she is dull and uninteresting. She compared her normal delivery to Henry Kissinger, who is noted for his understated, monotonous style. For a recent Christmas special, her news director told her to "jazz up" her delivery to fit the mood of the show. Not knowing how to do this, she forced an artificial delivery that she said sounded like a used car commercial. She was changing pitch and rate so much she lost all her credibility and sounded foolish. Without any training in how to change stress and intonation effectively, this can be the result.

Finding Meaning-Laden Words

The first step in developing a process to increase stress and intonation correctly is to find the meaning-laden words in your copy. This assumes, of course, that you do not plan to commit the greatest sin of broadcast delivery, which is to "rip and read" your copy on the air without a practice read-through. Unless you are on the air live during a disaster or a rapidly changing news event, no story should ever be read cold off the news wire or straight from a writer. To rip and read shows a lack of respect for your professional craft and for your audience. Even if a quick read-through is all you have time for before you go on the air, you owe that to your listeners.

Read through your copy out loud (you never help your delivery by reading broadcast copy silently) and look for meaning. On the first read-through you should use a pencil to mark the meaning-laden words. You might want to underline them or circle each one. Meaning-laden words are exactly what the name implies: words that carry meaning. In the sentence, "The quick brown fox jumped over the fence," the words "fox," "jumped," and "fence" carry the meaning. It is nice to know that the fox was quick and brown, but it is not imperative to the meaning. If you read this sentence with your stress on "quick," "brown," and "over," your listener would no doubt be confused.

Reading and marking copy should become routine for all broadcasters.

Courtesy of WWJ Radio, Detroit, MI   Courtesy of KSL–TV, Salt Lake City, UT

I use several examples to illustrate this idea for my clients. One example happens in thousands of homes each night. If I go into my living room at seven o'clock and switch on the television for the evening news, I will most likely then go into the kitchen and begin dinner. I cannot hear every word of the news, but I want to hear the meaning-laden words. If I hear "accident," "Gaithersburg," and "two injured," my interest will be piqued because I live in the area mentioned. I will go to the television to see the rest of the story.

This example would also be true if I were driving and listening to the radio. I may become distracted by any number of things, but as a broadcaster, you need to pull me into your story by stressing the meaning-laden words.

Another way to think of this concept is to visualize the lighting in a television studio. "Fill" and "key" lighting are two main types used in television. While the fill gives general illumination, the key lighting emphasizes certain people. It pulls those people out from the rest of the set, just as stressing certain words pulls them out from the rest of the sentence.

You can also think of a mountain range. When looking at the range, certain peaks rise above the rest. You see a fairly solid line of mountains with a few peaks standing out. As you read copy and stress the meaning-laden words, you are pulling them out just like the mountain peaks. You are making them stand above the rest by stressing them in a certain way. Your first task, however, is to find these words.

You should read through your copy looking for words that carry meaning. There is no easy formula. The meaning-laden words are not always the nouns and verbs. In this sentence, "Another attack by a pit bull dog has sent an elderly woman to the hospital," the modifiers "pit bull" are important to the meaning. You could find that an adverb is important, such as "continuously" in this sentence: "The gunman was continuously shooting, which made any rescue operation impossible." You will usually find that function words do not receive stress. These include prepositions, pronouns, conjunctions, and articles. This is not a hard and fast rule, however. Consider this sentence: "The boy was found in the hole and not beside it." The prepositions "in" and "beside" are important.

A close reading of your copy is the only way to seek out the meaning-laden words. Once you have marked your copy for these words you should have an outline of your story. A robbery story, for example, might give you these meaning-laden words: teenager, shotgun, fast food restaurant, suburban Detroit. Without reading the entire story, you have a good sense of what it says when you read the meaning-laden words.

Pausing for Breath and Meaning

Another initial step in creating a conversational delivery by marking your script involves deciding where you plan to pause. We have all heard broadcasters who pause at inappropriate places. If the sentence above were divided in this manner, it would lose meaning: "Another attack by a pit / bull dog has sent an elderly woman to the hospital." Many times inappropriate pauses come from the rip and read problem. If you have not read over your copy out loud, you are using guesswork when it comes to pausing. Other times, broadcasters pause inappropriately because they run out of air (see Chapter 1). You should mark your breath pauses so that you do not deplete your air supply as you are reading.

When marking your copy, use a double slash mark to designate a longer pause and a single slash mark for a short catch-breath and also for a quick pause with no intake of air. Double slash marks are often found at periods and when you go to a sound bite or actuality. This is a time when you can take a fairly deep breath. Single slash marks might be found at commas, dashes, ellipses, or at any point where meaning would be helped by a pause.

Marking these pauses before you mark meaning-laden words is preferable if you have the time. This allows you to work with phrases, instead of entire sentences, when you are looking for meaning. A phrase is a group of words between two slash marks. You might have two phrases in this sentence: "Another attack by a pit bull dog / has sent an elderly woman to the hospital." At the slash mark, you would take a catch-breath.

If your copy is written well, you will generally have at least one meaning-laden word in each phrase. In the sentence above you might pull out "attack," "pit bull dog," "woman," and "hospital." Those words carry the essential meaning of the sentence. It is easier to find these words when you work with the short phrases between slash marks.

Ways to Stress Words

Once you have decided where you want to pause and what words carry meaning, you are ready to make some choices about what you plan to do with your voice to pull out your meaning-laden words and verbally underline them for your listener. You will look at each meaning-laden word and decide what you want to do with your voice to stress each word.

You may have heard broadcasters talk about "punching" words to emphasize them. When my clients say they punch words, they usually mean they get louder on those words and possibly go up in pitch. Using this method alone causes problems, however, because it sets up a predictable, singsong delivery. In conversation, we do more with our voice than increase volume and go up in pitch. Incorporating a variety of stress and intonation methods will make your delivery sound more natural and conversational.

Intonation

Use of changes in our pitch in speech is called intonation. We use pitch changes within entire sentences to signal certain meanings, and within words to give them individual significance.

There are two basic patterns of intonation we use for sentences. Our normal intonation pattern calls for us to go down in pitch at the ends of sentences. This includes questions that begin with an interrogative (how, when, where, which, what, who, whose, whom, why). If you say, "How are you?" you go down in pitch at the end of the question. Try saying this sentence, listening to your pitch: "I had a good time." If you said it as a statement, you went down in pitch on "time" to indicate a complete thought. Now say it as a question: "I had a good time?" You should notice that since there was no interrogative to indicate a question, you went up in pitch on "time." Rising intonation in our language indicates a yes-no question or suggests uncertainty, insecurity, doubt, hesitancy, or an incomplete thought.

We also use pitch changes within sentences on certain words, and this is what is important for the process you will use to mark your script. Generally, in our language, for the most emphasized word in any phrase, our voices go up in pitch. Once you know your meaning-laden words, you should look at each one and decide if a pitch change would be an appropriate way to stress that word, and what pitch change is best.

There are three ways to use pitch for specific words. You can go up in pitch as you did in the above question without an interrogative, and you can go down in pitch as you do at the end of most sentences. Going down in pitch usually indicates finality or seriousness. If you say, "Three persons were killed in the accident," you would most likely go down in pitch on "killed." A sentence such as, "There were two survivors of the accident," would require a choice on your part. "Two survivors" could either go up or down in pitch, and either would be effective.

You can also use a circumflex intonation, which means you go up-down-up on a word or down-up-down. In our language, this intonation pattern indicates doubt or suspicion. Say this sentence and practice the circumflex intonation on the word "refused": "The CEO refused to be interviewed by our reporter." By alternating your pitch on "refused" you can indicate that something suspicious is going on with this executive.

When using a pitch change, you can glide up in pitch or you can step up. A glide up means that you begin the word at the same pitch as the previous word, but you go up in pitch as you say the word. A step up involves a clean pitch change from one word to the next (see Phonation Warm-Ups 7–10 in Chapter 2).

Duration

We also vary the length of words and syllables to stress them. If you said, "It was the biggest ice cream soda I ever ate," you probably stretched out the word "biggest." Stretching words out gives them more significance. This technique is very effective for numbers and figures. If a huge crowd turned out for a rally, you might say, "There was a record attendance of twenty-thousand people." Saying "twenty-thousand" slowly will impress the listener with the number.

Speeding up our speech can be effective as well. In the sentence, "The trial suffered still another set-back," it would be effective to speed up "still another set-back." You could also slow it down to make a point that the trial is dragging on. The choice would be up to you. Try saying this sentence both ways and see which sounds better to you.

Using variations in duration to emphasize certain words can be just as effective as variations in pitch. Changes in pitch or duration of words makes your meaning-laden words stand out from the rest, which helps your listener understand your story.

Volume

If you remember the last time you were angry about something, it may be easy to recall what an increase in volume is like. You may have said, "I said no!" On the word "no," you probably raised your volume.

For some broadcasters, increasing volume is their primary way of stressing words. These are the broadcasters who are difficult to listen to for any length of time. You feel as if you are being shouted at instead of reported to when this becomes a pattern.

Increasing volume is a legitimate way to stress words, but it should be used judiciously. It puts stress on your listener and on your throat. To increase your volume, you use more tension in the larynx. And this tension can lead to any number of vocal problems, as discussed in Chapter 2.

Pausing for Stress

In addition to pausing for meaning, you can also use pauses for stress. Pausing before and after a word or phrase pulls out an idea for the listener. It is as if the idea is suspended from the rest of the sentence. This might be used for a parenthetical phrase or clause such as, "The defendant, who is accused on ten counts, was not in the courtroom." It is natural to pause before "who" and after "counts."

You can use this method of pausing in other instances as well. You might say, "The county has a / restrictive limit / on new construction." By pausing in this way, the phrase "restrictive limit," is stressed.

A Method for Marking Scripts

Using the techniques described above (pitch, duration, volume changes, and pauses) you now have a basic method to improve stress and intonation in your broadcast copy. These techniques provide a way to superimpose a natural, conversational delivery on a very artificial process. You will be able to verbally underline your meaning-laden words for your listener just as you do in normal conversation.

This process can be used to mark every piece of copy you are given to read. Figure 12 outlines how the method can be used.

The copy marking method as presented here is only a starting point, however, for what should become a personal shorthand for you. In Figure 13 you see how this method looks when used on copy. I tell clients I hope that if I saw their copy a year after they worked through this method with me I would not recognize their markings. You should streamline the method to fit your needs.

It is important to remember as you go through the marking process that any story can be marked in a number of different ways and still be effective. There is no set way to mark each story. While I might choose to stretch out the phrase "Ten Most Wanted" in the last sentence in Figure 13, you might want to go down in pitch. The

Marking Teleprompter copy aids delivery.
Courtesy of KSL–TV, Salt Lake City, UT

choice is a personal one, but the important thing is to verbally underline the meaning-laden words by using a stress and intonation technique.

It is easy to use this method with copy for the sound booth as well as for Teleprompter copy that is hand fed into the machine. Unfortunately, the method cannot be used with most computer-generated Teleprompter copy. I have not found a computer program that allows for this marking system. Hopefully, in the future such a

---

Always perform the following procedure *in pencil* on your copy since you may find that you want to change markings:

1) Read through the copy out loud to check for difficult words.
   A. Look up the pronunciation of any difficult words.
   B. Write the phonetic transcription of difficult words on your copy.

2) Mark major breath pauses with // and minor breath pauses or pauses without an air intake with /.

3) Select the *meaning-laden* words to stress. Mark stressed words (usually at least one in each phrase) with the appropriate symbol given in Figure 12. (A phrase is a group of words between breath pauses.)

4) Reread copy out loud to check stress pattern.

5) Practice copy out loud as many times as possible.

program will be developed. If you have a computer-generated Tele-prompter, you may have to rely on spaces, dashes, and other typing techniques to develop a marking system.

Broadcast Copy Preparation Method for Stress and Intonation

This procedure may seem tedious and technical at first, but with practice, you will devise your own shorthand markings. The process can be integrated into the read-through of your copy.

When you begin working with this method, you should stick to the approach given here. As you progress with it, you will develop a personal marking method that will be much faster. You will find that the marking method is very tedious at first. It might take you thirty minutes to mark one page of copy. The usual response I get from clients is that there is no way this can ever work with the deadlines of a normal day.

Any new process is very technical at first. Remember when you first learned to drive a car? You may have thought that process would never be comfortable. What my clients find is that the more they practice this method of marking their script for meaning, the faster it becomes. Practice should be done initially in your non-work hours (see Stress and Intonation Warm-Ups). Do not expect to be able to read through this chapter and begin marking your on-air copy the same day.

I always caution clients against trying to use a marking method immediately. One anchor at a top market did not listen to my warning and almost lost her job when she tried to learn the method on the air. Her news director called her in and wanted to know what had happened. She was stumbling over words and sounded awful. This may be the result if you rush this process.

You should spend weeks, even months, getting comfort-able with a marking process. Once you are comfortable with it, you will hear tremendous improvement. The client whose delivery for a Christmas special sounded like a used car commercial found this

---

Figure 12
Vocal Methods for Stressing Words

1. Inflection up	The court has refused to vote.
2. Inflection down	The court has refused to vote.
3. Circumflex inflection*	The court has refused to vote.
4. Increase in volume	The court has <u>refused</u> to vote.
5. Pausing before & after words or phrases	The court has /refused/ to vote.
6. Stretching words out**	The court has refused to vote.
7. Saying words faster	The court has refused to vote.

*In American speech, circumflex inflection indicates doubt or suspicion.

**This is especially effective for numbers to give them added significance.

---

method gave her the confidence to abandon her monotone. She could use her voice to enhance meaning with the knowledge that she was emphasizing the correct words. For her, the method became part of her routine almost immediately, and she was using it on the air after practicing only a few weeks.

Figure 13
Sample Broadcast Copy Marked for Delivery

Three-thousand people in the Washington,

D.C., area were notified they had won two

free tickets to the Redskins' football

game.// About 100 of them showed up today

at the Convention Center for the tickets

and a pre-game brunch,/ but they were

thrown for a loss:// U.S. marshals and

police sprang their trap and arrested

them all as fugitives.// Some were wanted

for burglary, robbery or murder.// Two of

those caught in the sting were on the

local list of/Ten Most Wanted. //

Reprinted with permission from *Writing Broadcast News,* Mervin Block, Bonus
Books, Inc., 1987.

Examples of Script Marking Methods

Personalized marking methods have been used by both novice and
veteran broadcasters for years. Edward R. Murrow had a personal
marking style, which is illustrated in the news lead below, provided
by one of his former writers, Ed Bliss (see Figure 14). Bliss relates

Edward R. Murrow in wartime London where his coverage began
with the effective use of a pause: "This . . . is London."

Courtesy of CBS News

Figure 14
Edward R. Murrow Copy

Wednesday — February 6, 1952

This is the News —

The British have a new Queen.   King George the Sixth died in his sleep

last night at the age of 56.   His daughter, Queen Elizabeth, is due in

London tomorrow, (flying back from Kenya.)   Here is a recorded report from

Howard K. Smith in London, telling us how Her Majesty's subjects reacted

to the news.

TAPE:

Courtesy of Ed Bliss and Mrs. Edward R. Murrow

how Murrow always used a #2 yellow pencil to mark his script before each radio broadcast of "Edward R. Murrow—The News" (1947–1959). Bliss reports that Murrow would spend around ten minutes marking and rehearsing a six minute news summary. Bliss explains that Murrow used the exaggerated commas shown in Figure 14 as slash marks ". . . to feed the people a fact at a time." Regular commas indicated a slight pause. Murrow also often used a pause before verbs that he wished to emphasize. He used parentheses to set off phrases for meaning as well as underlining for emphasis. Murrow made few editorial changes in his scripts, according to Bliss, but he spent his preparation time deciding how to use his voice to enhance the meaning of the copy.

Brian Olson, News Director, KBMT–TV in Beaumont, Texas, teaches his staff a marking method that uses symbols in a different way (see Figure 15). Olson explains:

> Nothing fancy about the markings really. The
> key words are underlined for emphasis. The
> stronger the line, the stronger the emphasis. Ditto

Figure 15
Brian Olson Copy

NEWSOURCE EXTRA 2-14-90 10p bdo

VTR EXTRA/MONITOR.............

IMAGINE...

LIVING AND WORKING

IN A STEEL TUBE..

~~LESS~~ *LESS* THAN THREE

HUNDRED FEET LONG..

LESS THAN FORTY

FEET WIDE.

WITH YOU ARE

ONE HUNDRED ~~~~ AND FIFTY

OTHER PEOPLE.

THERE ARE NO WINDOWS

AND NO SUNLIGHT....

AND NO FRESH AIR

FOR PERIODS OF UP

TO THREE MONTHS

OR MORE.

THIS IS WHAT

LIFE IS LIKE

ABOARD A NUCLEAR

ATTACK SUBMARINE.

TONIGHT IN PART

TWO OF HIS SPECIAL

ASSIGNMENT

NEWSOURCE EXTRA

DISSOLVE FULL SCREEN CONT SIL

SERIES..."AMERICA'S

SILENT ~~~~ SERVICE"...

BRIAN OLSON SHOWS

US WHAT IT'S LIKE

TO WORK AND LIVE

ABOARD ~~~~.

THE GURH-NARD...

Courtesy of Brian Olson, News Director, KBMT–TV, Beaumont, TX for pauses. More "dots" .... a longer pause. What makes it all work is subtlety. The best changes in inflection and tone are always the subtle ones.

Other tips: For on-air work, always be on-set at least ten minutes before air. This allows you to relax, take a few sips of water and read through your copy at least twice. And read it aloud! So many anchors read their copy to themselves, then fumble all over the place when they get on the air.

Note that in this copy, we used the phonetic spelling of Gurnard (Gurh-nard). If there is the remotest chance of mispronunciation, always "spell it out!"

So I suggest subtlety and relaxation mixed with a large dose of "out loud" preparation. This is always a successful mix.

You can see that the markings used at KBMT are much more streamlined than the ones presented in Figure 12. Like Murrow's markings, they have been refined into a system that is fast and efficient. Your marking method should evolve as well. At first it will seem slow and technical to perform, and your delivery will sound slow and technical as well. As you continue to practice the technique, however, your own system and style will emerge.

Effective Use of Rate for Broadcast Delivery

Rate is an area that many broadcasters find confusing. They feel they deliver their copy too slowly, and when they speed up they get too fast. This is a common area of concern, because rate is very difficult to monitor on your own. I recently told a client to double her rate as she read a story for me. She thought that was ridiculous advice until she listened to the recording of her delivery at the faster rate. What had been a plodding delivery and a dull story suddenly became interesting.

Our rate of speaking is determined in many ways by our speech models. If your parents talk rapidly, you will most likely talk rapidly. If you come from a large family where you had to talk fast to be heard, you will have a rapid rate. On the other hand, a quiet, calm childhood may have produced a slow rate of speaking.

In broadcasting, control of rate is important, and reveals your sense of involvement and interest in a story. In your private life, it is acceptable to answer the phone with a slow, low-energy voice if you feel bad. For broadcasting, you must not let your moods show in your delivery. If you feel bad, you have to cover it up with a consistent rate and the sense of involvement that comes through marking your copy for meaning.

Appropriate Rates

Normally we read out loud at between 145 and 180 words per minute (wpm). The most comfortable speed is around 150 to 175 wpm (to learn your rate see Focus on Stress and Intonation). Our speaking rate is somewhat slower than our reading rate. Most of us speak at around 160 wpm or less. This is probably because we use more pauses and stretch words out more when we are talking. One contradiction to this is certain radio formats that call for very rapid-fire, extemporaneous delivery. In these instances, radio deejays may talk at 200 wpm or more.

When broadcasting, you can use rate to help verbally emphasize the mood of your story (see Table 2). A serious, sad story would be read more slowly than a kicker. Adjusting your rate makes the mood of the piece clearer for your listener.

It is often helpful to make a note in the margin of your copy that indicates the mood of each story (see Chapter 6). One client told me she likes to put the mood at the bottom of the page preceding each story. In this way, she can adjust her mood and rate as she turns her page of copy. It is all too easy to begin a sad story with a rapid rate before you realize the gravity of the piece. It is hard to adjust your rate and mood after you have begun a story.

Table 2
Rate Continuum

145 wpm	160 wpm	180 wpm
Material that is		
SAD	EXPOSITORY	LIGHT
SERIOUS	DESCRIPTIVE	HAPPY
GRAVE	UNEMOTIONAL	HUMOROUS
TECHNICAL		
COMPLICATED		

Components of Rate

Pauses have a great deal to do with overall rate. Two important components of rate are the number of pauses and the length of pauses. If you mark your pauses with slash marks, you will be able to gauge the number of pauses. The more you pause, the slower your delivery rate will be.

Another factor of rate that is more difficult to monitor is the duration of syllables. We vary the rate of syllable production based on the importance of the word and our natural speech pattern. Speech in a Southern accent is considered slow because Southerners tend to give more duration to their vowel sounds. By stretching out the vowels, the rate slows down. A Northerner or Midwesterner. might clip the vowel sounds, which would speed up their speech. Tape recording your delivery and monitoring the duration of syllables will help you become aware of your syllable production.

By marking your script, you can also monitor the words and phrases that you have decided to stretch out for meaning. If you find in a page of copy you are stretching out six or eight words, you will know that the delivery rate will be slow.

Focus on Stress and Intonation

Here is a summary of the main points involving stress and intonation for broadcast speech.

1. Most broadcast delivery is done in an artificial environment that eliminates feedback from the communication situation.

2. In normal speech, we use variations in pitch, rate, duration, and pauses to make our speech interesting and to reinforce meaning.

3. Our pitch goes down at the ends of sentences that are statements and in questions that begin with interrogatives.

4. Our pitch goes up at the ends of yes-no questions because there is no interrogative to signal the question. Going up in pitch also suggests uncertainty, insecurity, doubt, hesitancy, or an incomplete thought.

5. For broadcast speech, we can use variations in pitch, rate, duration, and pauses to give this artificial situation a natural sound.

6. Normal broadcast speech rate when reading copy ranges from 145 to 180 wpm. Rate should be adjusted to reinforce mood.

A) It is sometimes difficult for an individual to gauge the amount of stress and intonation used in broadcast work. For this reason, it is a good idea to tape record yourself reading some copy and ask a friend, a voice coach or teacher, or your news director to review the tape with you. Often when we think our pitch is rising, it is too subtle for others to detect. If this is the case, refer to the Phonation Warm-ups for ways to improve your pitch variation (see Chapter 2). Likewise, a loud volume to us may seem soft to someone else. Volume must be judged by a listener. Tape record this story using your normal broadcast delivery and review it with a critic you have selected:

> A new study says children who
> become hooked on television at an
> early age often become teenagers
> who are overweight. And the
> study by two Boston doctors
> reports that the more time
> these teens spend watching T-V,
> the more weight they put on--
> making them truly heavy viewers.
>
> Reprinted with permission from *Writing Broadcast News,* Mervin Block, Bonus Books, Inc., 1987.

B) Rate is also a difficult component of delivery to monitor without a conscious effort. The AP wire copy given below has a double slash mark at 150 words. Single slash marks indicate groups of ten words before and after the 150 mark. Read this section at your normal rate, timing your delivery. Mark the point you reach after reading for exactly sixty seconds. Next, count up or back from the 150 mark to where you stopped reading to calculate how many words per minute you read. If you find you were reading as slowly as 140 wpm, reread the section, trying to speed up. If you read above 180 wpm, try to slow down. This is an unemotional story that should be read with a normal delivery of around 150 to 175 wpm.

> A prisoner being taken by
> federal marshals from Alabama
> to California, bolted out of a
> moving plane's emergency exit
> after landing on Saturday and
> fled into the darkness,
> authorities said.

U.S. Marshal Stuart Earnest said the escapee, 44-year-old Reginald D. Still, was en route from a federal hospital in Talladega, Alabama, to Sacramento, California, where he was scheduled to go on trial on a charge of interstate transportation of a stolen motor vehicle.

Earnest said the plane contained 44 prisoners when it touched down at Will Rogers World Airport. No other prisoners tried to escape, he said.

Still wearing handcuffs and shackles, he leaped out of the plane's emergency exit, onto a wing and then the tarmac as the plane was braking, / the marshal said.

One of the eight security people on / the plane jumped out to chase the escapee, Earnest said. //

Federal marshals and local, county and state authorities fanned out / across the airport property, southwest of Oklahoma City, in the / search.

Prisoners are normally transported by a Boeing 727, but a backup, a Convair 580 propeller, was being used Saturday because the jet was being repaired, authorities said.

The U.S. marshal's service routinely transports prisoners

every other day to courts and
penitentiaries around the
country. The transportation
program is based in Oklahoma
City, and prisoners on
overnight trips often are
housed overnight at a federal
correctional facility in El
Reno, 30 miles west of here.

Reprinted with permission from *Writing Broadcast News,* Mervin
Block, Bonus Books, Inc., 1987.

C) To feel the effect of no feedback on communication,
look just above someone's head when you are talking or turn and
face the wall. Ask the person not to respond verbally while you tell
them about an interesting event. You will notice that without feedback, natural conversational delivery is impaired. Many people feel
the same way when talking on the telephone because they are not
making eye contact with their listener.

Stress and Intonation
Warm-Ups

Discovering that your stress and intonation are not appropriate and
deciding to change them is not always enough. You must know how
to change stress and intonation to enhance meaning. The method
described in Figure 12 gives you a way to do this.

When you first begin practicing this method, it will seem
time-consuming and technical. For the method to work, you must
continue to practice until you feel comfortable using the method and
your delivery sounds natural and conversational. Practice every day,
marking copy and tape recording your delivery.

Keep in mind that this method is based in meaning, and is
not simply a technique or a delivery trick. If you have decided where
your meaning-laden words are, you need not fear that you will fall
into a set delivery pattern. Every story will be different based on the

meaning. You will be reading for sense and not for sound. You should be able to develop a delivery that does not sound forced or insincere.

Remember also that there are many ways each sentence can be marked. The important thing is to pull out the meaning-laden words for your listener. Where you decide to pause and how you decide to stress a word or phrase is a personal decision that should be based in meaning and your delivery style.

1) In each of the following sentences, go through the marking method as described in Figure 12. First mark pauses if there are any, and then find the meaning-laden words. Once you have selected the words, decide how you plan to stress each one and mark each with the appropriate symbol.

- Two men are dead and a third

  in stable condition after a

  multiple shooting in

  Gainesville last night.

- Authorities are still

  investigating a robbery in the

  southeast part of the city

  this morning.

- The Shelby County Mental

  Health Association will

  provide trained counselors to

  help locate available housing

  for the homeless this winter.

- 19 of 30 people sought in connection with the large scale cocaine ring, which operated out of the Pizza Shop on west Main, were arrested last night.

- A commuter aircraft on final approach and a private plane collided over the Knoxville airport this afternoon injuring ten people.

2) Once you have practiced the marking method on sentences, expand your practice to include complete stories.

A new study says the people more likely to get heart attacks are short. That applies, apparently, to men and women. In the study, men under five-foot-seven had about 70 percent more heart attacks than those over six-one.

The study was done at a Boston hospital. But researchers

warn that being tall is no guarantee of escaping heart trouble--and urge people to exercise and watch their cholesterol.

A Jeep flipped over on Interstate 90 in Harborcreek Township today, and a passenger was thrown out. A Life Star helicopter flew him to Saint Vincent's Hospital, where he's listed in good condition. He's a tourist from Rome, Italy: Robert Amirian, 32 years old. A state trooper says the Jeep was going too fast for the slippery pavement.

Two men jailed in Chicago on a murder charge for more than a year have been freed, and a man already in prison has been indicted for murder. The victim was robbed and shot last year on the Granville El platform.

Today, charges against Derrick Hamilton and Eugene Williams were dropped.

A U-S Navy plane caught fire over the Mediterranean today, and the five-man crew bailed out. Navy helicopters rescued them--unhurt--from the sea near Cyprus. But the burning plane, an E-two-C Hawkeye, kept going. So for safety--or security--a Navy fighter plane shot it down. The Hawkeye had been on early-warning duty supporting Allied relief work for the Kurds in northern Iraq.

A fire in a home at 2220 Perkins, Saginaw, has caused heavy damage. The owner, Ernest Belford, and his family were not home. Fire officials say some clothing had been too close to a water heater and was set on fire. It took firefighters two hours to put the fire out. No estimate yet

on damage.

Reprinted with permission from *Broadcast Newswriting: The RTNDA Reference Guide,* Mervin Block, Bonus Books, Inc., 1994.

I tell our staff to imagine they're telling the news to a close, personal friend or relative. It sounds silly to some, but it's served as a sure-fire way to enhance our product. Our listeners feel as though they're hearing what they need to know from a trusted, compassionate friend!

Dan Shelley
News Manager, KTTS AM/FM
Springfield, Missouri

The advice I give most often is: "understand and convey." Understand the emotions inherent in the copy and convey those emotions to the listener through your interpretation of the copy with your delivery. We aren't "delivering the news" to the masses. We're "telling a story" to one person at a time.

Dan Potter
News Director, WBAP News/talk 820
Fort Worth, Texas

News people do not understand the psychology of the broadcast microphone, how to speak to one person at a time who is listening and tell them the story.

Tom Fowler
News Director, WRLK–TV
Columbia, South Carolina

Sounding Conversational

Script marking and a consideration of rate as discussed in the last chapter are effective ways to improve on-air delivery. They provide a method for superimposing a conversational style onto a written text. Like a musical score, script marking can give you guidelines for delivery. But for some people, this method is not enough, and for others it is too technical. You may find that you want to augment the marking system or use a technique that will put you more in touch with talking with a person. My advice to broadcasters is to take a few seconds to PREP before each story. Using the mnemonic of PREP (see Figure 16) you can follow a step-by-step process that helps you talk with a person in a conversational style.

Figure 16
An Interpersonal Communication Approach to Broadcast Delivery

PERSON

ROOM

EMOTIONS

PLACE

Developing an
Interpersonal Style

All on-air people have been given the age-old advice to imagine they are talking to someone to improve their conversational quality. The problem is that it is hard to conjure up an image when you are facing a camera or the wall in a sound booth. It is not easy to hallucinate on command. Not many of us can turn a camera lens into someone's face without doing some preliminary work to make this possible. And even if we can, just seeing the face is not enough. What is really needed is the active feedback that is an integral part of normal conversation (see Figure 11 in Chapter 5).

When I ask clients to tell me who they are imagining they are talking with, I get very nebulous images such as "a young woman" or "someone sort of like my sister." I have also gotten very concrete images like "five hundred community leaders" or "all the people in the newsroom." These choices do not create the intimacy that is needed to develop an interpersonal communication event. What is needed is the well-developed image of a partner for communication.

P = Person

The first "P" in the word PREP stands for "Person." Like that age-old advice, the first step is to imagine a person. But this is not a vague image. Pick a real person with whom you are comfortable talking and can imagine vividly—a friend, neighbor, cousin, etc. The demographics of your station should help in this selection. Choosing an eighty-year-old grandmother does not fit most demographics. A thirty-five-year-old housewife might be more accurate. At the end of this chapter in Focus on Sounding Conversational you will find a checklist to help you select your Person.

Once you have made your choice, this is the Person with whom you will always speak when on the air. You may at some point want to select another Person if you move to another station or want a new approach, but it is important to be consistent. Changing your Person for each story or every few days will make it hard for you to create rapport instantly in your mind.

Once you have established rapport with your Person, you will be able to use interpersonal skills when reading from a script. You will be able to come through the electronic wall and really reach your listener. We all know how to talk to a friend, neighbor, or cousin. Our pitch might go up when we want to stress a word, and we might stretch some words out and say others faster. We do this naturally because of the feedback we get from our friend when we are talking. The listener may be nodding, smiling, or looking puzzled, which helps us vary our delivery. Creating a Person to talk with helps these same qualities become part of broadcast delivery.

Television and radio are very intimate communication encounters. Many people spend more time with their television or radio than they do with other people. They may even get physically closer to their television and radio than other people. The listeners must be talked with in a comfortable, conversational way. People do not want an announcer who sounds like he is talking to five hundred people. An important thing to remember is that in broadcasting you are always talking with one person as several million others eavesdrop. Good interpersonal communication sounds like you are talking with just one person in an enlarged conversational style. It is enlarged because you are more conscious of your breathing, resonance, and articulation. But it should still be conversational.

To enhance this feeling of talking with one person, you might even take a photograph of the person into the sound booth and talk to the photograph. This can help you keep the listener in mind. One of my clients imagined that the sound booth console was a breakfast bar and his person was sitting on the other side of the bar. Whatever works to help you envision the listener can be helpful. The listener is always the most important person in the broadcasting encounter. Vividly creating this Person in your mind creates a sense of interpersonal communication.

R = Room

The "R" in PREP will also help in this process. Once the Person has been selected, put that Person in a room—"R" stands for "Room." Selecting a friend or neighbor makes it easy to remember that Person in the Room where they would be watching television or listening to the radio. I know, for example, that my friend's television is in her kitchen. I can imagine what the Room looks like. I can see her sitting at the table, and I can even smell the coffee. All these sensual factors help me bring this Person to life.

We all do this every day when we talk on the telephone. If we call for airline reservations, for example, we imagine the office the agent is sitting in. We even imagine what the person looks like. Using our imaginations is something we all do well.

It will help you to use this skill in the sound booth. You will be able to really see the Person and imagine him or her in the Room where that Person would be listening or watching. This visualization may only take a few seconds, but it will help create a sense of talking with someone.

Visualization or creative imagery like this has been used in sports and theatre for years (see Chapter 7). Many sports figures spend time imagining they are hitting home runs or making three-pointers. Dancers see themselves leaping effortlessly across the stage. Broadcasters can use the same skill to create a Person with whom they can share their stories. Delivery should sound like a broadcaster is talking *with* this person instead of *at* a camera or microphone. Creating a vivid sense of the Person and putting him or her in a Room can make this possible.

E = Emotion

Another factor in interpersonal communication is emotion, which is what the "E" in PREP stands for. Using emotion in the news is a

Despite the surroundings of a studio, broadcasters must create the sense that they are talking with a person.

Courtesy of Army Broadcasting Service

controversial subject, but there is a difference between being impartial and insensitive. I hear too many anchors and reporters who have become so distanced from emotion they sound like robots.

It is never appropriate for a reporter or anchor to editorialize during a straight newscast. Showing emotion in a news story applies only to *universal emotions* and not controversial stories. A court case that is unresolved would not involve any emotion in the delivery. Likewise, a story about a possible scandal or alleged misconduct by an authority should be read without any emotional involvement. *Universal emotions* refer to emotions that all of us feel. This might apply to a story about children suffering, a family being killed in a fire, a plane crashing, or people starving. If no emotion is felt while delivering stories such as these, the broadcaster will sound cold and insensitive.

When I talk about portraying emotion, I mean a subtle feeling of emotion. In a sad story, tears or a break in the voice would not be appropriate. Portraying emotion in this situation might simply mean a slower rate and a softer tone of voice. A carefully placed pause can indicate a sense of emotion. Generally, for example, we talk faster, louder, and with a higher pitch when we are happy. We speak slower, with more pauses, softer, and with a lower pitch when we are sad.

The prevalence of video cassette recorders in almost every home has increased the need for broadcasters to be in touch with the emotions of what they are reading. There is an archival quality to news stories that did not exist before. A story about a tragic death or a lottery winner may be taped and viewed many times by the families and friends touched by the story. Before home VCRs were commonplace, news stories were not studied in detail. Now almost every family has some news story they are saving to show others. Broadcasters have a greater responsibility to be aware of the meaning and emotion of stories.

Even what may appear to be a routine statement often sounds more effective if it reflects some emotion. Consider the line, "We'll continue hourly updates on the progression of the hurricane throughout the evening." For a listener sitting in a beach house in the path of this hurricane, this is a very emotion-laden statement. Delivering this statement with a sense of concern will project the feeling that your station cares about its listeners.

I often hear anchors in the Washington, D.C., area reporting on another drug-related shooting death in the city as if it were a stock market report. Even if this is the five hundredth shooting of the year, it is still a death, and it deserves a delivery that shows that the on-air person understands the tragedy. This does not mean the anchor should become an actor. If you are going to reflect emotion in your delivery you really have to feel it. Audiences are very sensitive to forced emotion or fake sincerity. Putting emotion into stories means getting in touch with the *universal emotion* of the story and reflecting that with your voice.

Emotions run the gamut from joyful to tragic, happy to sad. It is important to analyze carefully the emotion of each story. I have clients who say all their stories are "serious." Using an umbrella term like this limits the possibilities for recognizing the subtle emotions in a story. You need to peel away the layers of emotion. There is a difference between a fire story where no one was killed, for example, and one with deaths. They are both serious, but the first is somber or grave, and the second is tragic or sad.

It is helpful to write the emotion of the story in the margin on the copy as a reminder. Stories may change emotion as they progress. Careful analysis is the only way to trace the progression of emotions. Listening to news headlines illustrates this. The first headline might deal with a tragic plane crash, followed by a frustrating traffic tie-up, and finishing with a joyful lottery winner headline. The anchor reading this would need to reflect these changes vocally (see Sounding Conversational Warm-Ups).

There are some techniques that will help integrate emotion into delivery. You can precede your countdown with a phrase like, "Jim, I have a really sad story to tell you. Three, two, one. . . ." This simple sentence using your Person will help capture the emotion before voicing. You can also talk to your Person for a few seconds about the upcoming story before you begin to record or to go live. Tell them what the emotion is and how it affects you to report on it. After doing this, you will be in the emotion when you read the story.

Using emotion can add a human quality to delivery, but remember that it needs to be a sincere, *universal emotion*. Faking emotion or editorializing with your delivery is never appropriate. It is as unethical to fake emotion as it is to fake an event for the news. In order to relate to stories with emotion, you have to let your human

Prepare for stand-ups by talking to your Person for a few seconds about the story before you begin.

Courtesy of WWCP–TV, Johnstown, PA

sensitivity come into play. This is not easy considering the tragic quality of many news events. But it is a necessity if you want to be a broadcaster who has rapport with listeners.

P = Place

The final "P" in PREP stands for "Place," which involves the place in which the listener imagines the reporter to be. This only applies to sound booth work, not to anchoring.

When most of us listen to television packages or radio stories, we imagine the reporter is on the scene. Most listeners have no idea that the reporter is really speaking to them from inside a foam-covered closet. Even though I know voicing is done in a sound booth, my immediate reaction is that the reporter is on the scene. The more a reporter can portray this feeling vocally, the more effective the voicing will be. There should be a "live" quality about the story.

The reporter is the listener's ears and eyes on the scene. The listener wants to feel there is an immediacy to the story, and that the reporter is watching it unfold. Listeners create this image just like we imagine the room in which the airline agent is seated when we talk on the telephone.

One of the best examples of this was told to me by Mike Freedman, the former managing editor for the broadcast division of United Press International. Mike said that for years UPI opened its newscasts with the phrase, "From the World Desk of United Press International. . . ." When people toured the UPI headquarters, they always wanted to see the "World Desk" where they thought the newscasts were done. Bill Ferguson, a veteran UPI executive, had to have a set built that was the "World Desk" so people could see it. Even though the news was never delivered from this desk, it created the reality the listener imagined.

A reporter's job is to create the feeling that he or she is on the scene. This is not easy to do and there are no real guidelines to help achieve this. In Focus on Sounding Conversational (see page 154), you will find a checklist to help. Broadcasters have to see past the foam-covered walls of the sound booth and remember what it felt like, smelled like, and sounded like on the scene.

When this sense of imagining works, the scene comes to life for the broadcaster and for the listener. It is like the difference between standing on the stage in the middle of the event instead of looking down from the balcony and reporting on it.

Becoming a Comfortable Communicator

Taking a few minutes to go through the steps of PREP before voicing can help create a sense of interpersonal communication with the listener. If broadcasters know who they are talking to and can bring that person to life in their minds, they can reach out to that listener. Feeling *universal emotions* and having a sense of where the listener imagines the broadcaster to be will complete a sense of communication.

In broadcasting today, the best newscasters are not necessarily the ones with the booming, deep voices like Ted Baxter or Jim Dial. The best newscasters are the ones who communicate with their listener. PREPPING before voicing can help achieve a sense of being a comfortable communicator.

Focus on Sounding Conversational

A) Here is a checklist to follow to help you select the Person with whom you wish to speak:

P = Person
1. Find out about the demographics of your audience. Who is your primary audience? Who is a typical listener?
2. Select a person who fits into your key demographic category.
   a. This person should *not* be a parent or your child or anyone with whom you might use a different vocal style.
   b. Select someone you know very well and with whom you feel comfortable talking.
3. Write the answers to these questions about your Person:
   a. How old is your Person?
   b. How interested is the Person in listening to the news?
   c. What type of feedback does your Person give you when you speak with him or her in person? Visualize the feedback.
4. Arrange to talk with this person if possible and observe his or her feedback as you talk.
5. If you want, get a photograph of your Person to help bring the Person to life in your mind.

R = Room
1. Find out where your Person usually watches or listens to the news.
2. Visit the Room if possible. This Room might be a living room, kitchen, office, or even a car.
3. Create a visual image of your Person in the Room. Take a photograph of the room if you find this helpful.
4. Get a sensual image of the Room.
   a. What smells are present?
   b. What is the temperature?
   c. What other noises are there?
   d. What lighting is used?
   e. Is your Person alone in the room? Are there other people? pets?

5. Write a visual and sensual description of your image of the room so that you can use it for reference.

B) **E = Emotion.** Here are some possible emotions to consider when you analyze the *universal emotions* of what you are reading. This is only a partial list to give you an idea of the different levels of emotions:

HAPPY	SAD	INTERESTED	ENCOURAGING
excited	sorrowful	intrigued	confident
inspired	tragic	curious	proud
optimistic	somber	fascinated	awed
joyful	disappointed	inquisitive	hopeful

C) **P = Place.** Use this checklist to establish a sense of the Place when you come back into the newsroom to voice a story:
  1. What time of day was it?
  2. What were the sensual feelings at the scene?
      a. What was the temperature?
      b. What smells were in the air?
      c. What sounds were there?
      d. Were many people around or was it isolated?
      e. How were the people feeling who were there (e.g., panicked, happy, sad, afraid)?
  3. What was the weather like?

Sounding Conversational Warm-Ups

1) If you find it is really difficult for you to portray any emotion with your voice, try reading children's stories out loud. Some good choices are *The Three Little Pigs, Cinderella, Snow White,* or *Bambi.* Really exaggerate the emotions. Better yet, read to a child. The child will let you know right away if you are not reading with enough emotion. A child wants to hear the fear in your voice when the story is scary and experience the joy of a happy ending.

2) You can practice emotion reading news copy. Take copy home and exaggerate the emotions. Let yourself laugh in a happy story and sound overly distraught in a sad one. This is for practice only, but it will help you push the parameters of what you can do with your voice in terms of emotion. You will want to pull back from the exaggeration in your on-air delivery.

3) When you are in someone's home, observe how they watch the news. Do they look at the screen of the television? Most studies indicate that viewers look at the screen less than fifty percent of the time. What makes a person look at the screen? Become aware of all the distractions broadcasters have to contend with when delivering a newscast.

4) Practice these headlines until you can distinguish the emotion of each one with your voice:

```
Topping the news headlines this
hour . . .

A commuter plane crashes into a
Birmingham neighborhood. Dozens
are believed dead . . .

The state school superintendent
unveils a new math program . . .

And a heaven-sent gift . . .
it's the day of the solar
eclipse.
```

5) Aircheck yourself at least once a week and listen to your use of emotion. Also gauge your connection with the listener. Have you created an intimate encounter? Have you come through the electronic wall? Weekly airchecks should be part of your professional routine.

Stress can be your worst enemy when it comes to on-air performance. It's impossible to remain conversational if your stress level is high. Relating to the viewer on a conversational level is the most important thing you can do.

Jeff Alan
News Director, WWCP–TV
Johnstown, Pennsylvania

Your delivery must be natural and your body relaxed because it always gets worse when you are nervous, hurried, or reading off-the-cuff.

Jeff Karnowski
News Director, KRCG–TV
Jefferson City, Missouri

Please, as an anchor, don't try to "sell" me on a story by overdoing. "Serve" me instead—make me comfortable with you. Make me want to invite you into my home.

Jay Mitchell
Assistant News Director,
WPEC–TV/WFLX–TV
West Palm Beach, Florida

Coping with Stress

If you work in television or radio news these days it is very hard NOT to be tense. There is a scene in the movie *Broadcast News* where a television anchor begins sweating profusely while delivering a newscast. Many on-air broadcasters can definitely relate to this scene!

There is no other profession that is more demanding than being on-air. Even a brain surgeon can take a break during surgery, but an anchor or reporter doing live work does not have that option. If a television or radio anchor begins getting tense during a newscast, that person has to be able to deal with it on live television or radio. There is no walking out of the studio or asking for a time-out.

A tense body means a tense voice. It is possible to learn every muscle in the throat and all the information available on how to improve vocal delivery, but nothing will help if you are tense. I have seen this problem with many clients.

One international network correspondent told me she suffered so severely from stress that she barely slept at night, ate no more than a few rushed bites of food a day, and used caffeine and sugar to keep going. Not surprisingly, she suffered headaches, had

The stressful demands of a live broadcast are a part of most broadcasters' workdays.

Courtesy of KTTS AM/FM, Springfield, MO

trouble breathing, and had repeated bouts of hoarseness. She was not even able to take a deep abdominal-diaphragmatic breath and was on the verge of hyperventilating all the time. Before any vocal progress could be made, she had to work on the chronic stress her body was experiencing.

The Importance of Coping with Stress

Like vocal exercises, stress control techniques should be part of every broadcaster's day. Other professionals, like actors, dancers, and singers, know the value of keeping their bodies fit and relaxed, and it is equally important for broadcasters.

News directors and general managers should recognize the effect of stress in the workplace as well. It is estimated that stress-related diseases account for seventy-five to ninety percent of visits to primary care doctors. Job stress is believed by many to be the *number one* adult health problem in this country. And these statistics are drawn from a cross section of jobs. If we consider the unrelenting stress of working in broadcast news with hourly deadlines and split-second timing, we begin to get an idea of how stress affects newsroom personnel.

The Physiological Response

Let's look at what stress really is. Basically, it is a feeling of being out of control—a feeling that at a particular moment you do not have control of your life.

What gives us this feeling of being out of control? It is the flight or fight response, which is a chain reaction of automatic bodily processes. The same reflexes that allowed our ancestors to run from attacking animals and fight to defend their tribes allow us to deal with deadlines and get interviews. Our body does not know the difference between an irate congressman and a saber-toothed tiger. Stress is stress.

When faced with stress, our brain releases a surge of adrenaline. This increases our blood pressure, makes our heart beat faster, and ups our oxygen intake. Blood rushes to our muscles, which makes the digestive system shut down. We begin to sweat, and our muscles tense. All of this increases our strength, gives us more energy, and makes our thinking clearer.

But it is meant to be an emergency response. This adrenaline is supposed to be used up by the stressful event. There should be a healthy cycle of arousal which leads to increased performance followed by fatigue, which forces us to rest and restore the body. We have all experienced this when we play a heated game of tennis or swim laps. We feel lots of energy which gets burned off and then the body wants to rest to regenerate (see Figure 17).

There is a place for healthy stress in the newsroom to help get you through a crisis, but the problem is that the hypothalamus in the brain takes all incoming messages and prepares the body for action. There is no discrimination. So a constant state of stress can

Figure 17
Stress Patterns

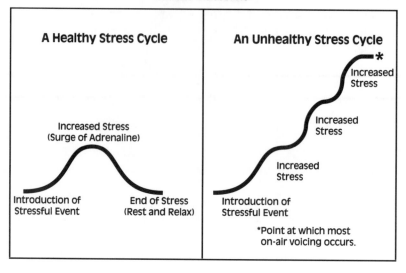

develop. Even if the actual physical release never happens, the body has been prepared. And our emotional state alone may place the body on alert. Being anxious or fearful or impatient may signal the brain that we are in danger and need a burst of adrenaline.

If there is uninterrupted stress as there often is in a newsroom, the body never has a chance to return to its relaxed state (see Figure 17). Chronic stress short-circuits the natural process. The effect is like a tape recorder stuck on fast-forward. The machine overheats and quickly burns out.

Unfortunately, the more stressed we are, the less we are likely to realize it. And many people become stress addicts and enjoy the high they get from the extra energy. But chronic stress keeps the body running at such an unnatural level that our organs can not function normally and regenerate as they should.

Panic Attacks

Stress can be more than just a slight inconvenience. One of the best-kept secrets in a newsroom is panic attacks. A panic attack is the ultimate response to too much stress. Many broadcasters have them and most tell me they have never told anyone else about them. The tension of working in broadcasting can produce symptoms as severe as panic attacks.

A panic attack is like the core meltdown of stress. It feels like someone pulled the emergency brake at eighty miles per hour. The body goes into a full-scale panic very quickly. In fact, a panic attack is the fastest and most complex bodily reaction. It is one of the most distressing experiences a person can go through. Many people think they are dying when they have a panic attack.

What does this feel like? Well, it may begin with a tingling feeling in your feet and move up the body. You begin to sweat all over and breathing becomes difficult. Your body may feel really cold or hot. You feel nauseated, your heart races, and you may get dizzy or your vision may begin to go black. One television anchor felt she wanted to run off the set. Another said her mind would go blank, and she would forget where she was. Others begin sweating profusely just like the scene from *Broadcast News.*

Panic disorders affect three million people in this country, and most people affected are overachievers, perfectionists, and controlling individuals. Therefore, it is not surprising that many broadcasters are victims of panic attacks.

Broadcasters at every level of the business have had panic attacks while on the air. These include veteran network correspondents as well as anchors. It is much more common than people realize because it is usually suffered in silence. News directors are often the last to know that someone on their staff is suffering from severe stress.

Negative Effects of Chronic Stress

The toll chronic stress takes on the body is devastating. A stressed-out person may suffer physical symptoms, emotional symptoms, or both. The first reactions might include exhaustion, irritability, irregular breathing, sleep disturbances, or possibly nervous mannerisms like nail biting and finger tapping. These may progress into headaches, back pain, chronic stomach upsets, and skin rashes. As the stress continues, ulcers may develop as well as artery and heart problems.

Stress affects the voice in very significant ways. Every aspect of the voice—breathing, phonation, resonance, and articulation—suffers when a person is tense.

The first place many broadcasters feel stress is in their breathing. Stress inhibits breathing, which affects vocal production because breathing is the energy for speech (see Chapter 1). Poor breathing results in low vocal energy or a tired, monotone sound. It also limits air supply, which can make it difficult to finish sentences without lots of pauses to breathe. And you may hear audible intakes of air when the person stops to breathe. A glottal fry can also happen, which is a popping sound at the ends of sentences when the air supply is low.

I find that poor posture brought on by stress often contributes to breathing difficulties. There is a body position called the startle response which is a posture we go into when we are startled—we pull our shoulders up toward our ears and tense our stomach and chest muscles. All of this makes comfortable abdominal-diaphragmatic breathing difficult. This posture affects breathing, which affects the voice (see Focus on Coping With Stress on page 178).

Pitch also rises when the body is tense. The voice gets higher and higher as tension increases. Resonance is restricted when the body is tense as well. If the jaw is clenched and the throat and mouth muscles are tense, the voice is more likely to sound high-pitched and thin. Holding the mouth in a tense position also limits articulation, making it harder to sound precise when speaking.

As if all these physical problems were not enough, there are also emotional reactions to tension. Chronic stress makes it more difficult to think clearly. Radio and television reporters find live work difficult because they cannot focus their thinking. They have trouble making a transition from the hectic schedule of deadlines and interviews to the focused, one-on-one demands of a live broadcast. Stress affects anchors and reporters reading copy as well. Stressed broadcasters tend to read faster and lose the vocal expressiveness needed to sound conversational. They have a difficult time focusing on the listener because they are so aware of their own stress level.

Every aspect of voice is affected by the level of stress a person is experiencing. That is why it is so important to stress-proof your life as much as possible.

The usual stress of broadcasting increases in dangerous locations such as the one this Armed Forces Network correspondent faced in Sarajevo, Bosnia.

Courtesy of Army Broadcasting Service

How to Stress-Proof Your Life

There are three aspects of life that can be adjusted to help relieve stress. The first is diet and environment. The second is exercise. And the third involves conscious relaxation. In addition to these three areas, it is important to look at the health of the workplace.

Environment

There is not a lot you can do about the general ambience of a newsroom. There will always be phones ringing, television monitors and scanners blaring, and people talking. But studies have shown that plants and pictures help create a less stressful environment. They provide something to look at besides the usual papers and printouts. Incandescent desk lamps instead of overhead fluorescents have also been shown to reduce stress.

Another way to improve the work space is to post affirmations. Something simple like, "I am in control of my life," or "Life is not an emergency," may help break the tension of the newsroom. When life is at its craziest, just thinking of one of these phrases will help.

It is important to consider the stress level in the studio as well. I am amazed at the unprofessional activities that go on during broadcasts in television and radio studios. These run the gamut from squirting people with water guns during commercial breaks to working puzzles and telling jokes. I have seen television co-anchors engage in shouting matches every time they go to a commercial. These activities contribute to a more stressful environment. You may think that clowning around during a break will help lessen stress, but the effect is a loss of focus. Staying focused on the newscast by reading the upcoming copy out loud during commercial breaks is the best stress reliever. It may be necessary to alert floor directors or engineers to the importance of creating a professional environment in the studio. Everyone should contribute to the quality of the newscast by concentrating on their jobs. They owe that to the listeners.

Diet

One aspect of daily life that is very controllable is what is consumed by the body (see Figure 18). Diet and smoking have a direct effect on stress. Many of the foods we rely on in times of stress actually make the condition worse. They give an instant energy burst, but in the long run they add to chronic stress.

Caffeine has a strong effect on the amount of adrenaline in the body. It mimics stress by stimulating the adrenal glands and the heart. Add sugar to that and the problem is compounded because sugar affects the blood sugar level. Drinking coffee and sodas all day accompanied by snacks or junk food full of sugar, and the adrena-

---

Figure 18

Here is a quick checklist to determine if your diet or eating habits are increasing your stress level:

1. Do you usually do polyphasic activities? Do you do two or three other things while you are eating, like reading, listening to the radio, watching television monitors, editing copy?

2. Do you eat in less than thirty minutes?

3. Do you often skip meals, especially lunch, because you just do not have the time to eat?

4. Do you drink more than two cups of tea or coffee or caffinated sodas a day?

5. Do you drink more than two alcoholic beverages a day?

6. When you need an energy boost, do you grab a candy bar or something high in sugar or caffeine?

7. Do you eat foods high in fat?

Answering *YES* to any of these questions means you are adding stress to what is already a stressful work day.

---

line level, which is already high, gets even higher, and the body gets even tenser (see Figure 17).

Many broadcasters do not eat enough to keep their blood sugar at a constant level. Undereating deprives the brain of essential nutrients and asks your body to function without fuel. None of us would drive our automobile with the gas tank on empty, and we should not ask our body and mind to operate without fuel. It is important to take care of your body and stay in training considering the demands of the news business. Eating complex carbohydrates and proteins will provide the steady energy it takes to do your job well.

Substitute healthy snacks such as fruit and raw vegetables for junk food. Keep a supply of these snacks in your desk to avoid the run to the vending machines. Also, stay away from fatty foods, which may take five to seven hours to digest. The digestion process takes blood to the stomach and a sluggishness will result. The brain can not function as efficiently when digestion has deprived it of blood. Eating fruit, which takes less than an hour to digest, or bread, which takes one to three hours, will help you stay alert.

Another diet consideration is how often you eat during the day. I have had many clients tell me they eat only one meal a day. This is usually a large dinner when they get home at night. They wonder why when they sit down to anchor at six o'clock they usually have a bad headache. Our bodies need food throughout the day to avoid the effects of low blood sugar, which can include headaches, nervousness, and dizziness. Your stress level will be higher if your body has not gotten enough food throughout the day to keep your blood sugar at an appropriate level.

Some clients like to eat small meals throughout the day to keep their energy up. This is ideal and can be done without any weight gain if you select your foods wisely. For expert advice, check with a nutritionist. With proper exercise and a good diet, you can eat what you want throughout the day and sustain your optimum energy level.

Eating a good breakfast high in complex carbohydrates like breads, cereals, fruits, and whole grains is important to have the energy to perform well during the morning hours. It is also important to eat lunch. This is often skipped by reporters in the field. I suggest to clients that they take foods with them that are easy to eat like granola bars, fruit, and breads so that they are not tempted to skip lunch.

And stay away from caffeine. The best alternative is water because it has no calories and keeps the vocal tract moist and healthy (see Chapter 2). For warm drinks try herbal or decaffeinated tea or if you cannot live without your morning coffee at least limit it to one cup and then switch to decaf coffee.

The brain is seventy-five percent fluid, and brain function is affected by dehydration. (For the amount of water the body needs, see Chapter 2, "Vocal Hydration.") Undereating and poor hydration of the body both affect performance. You will help your voice and your thinking ability by drinking lots of water and eating healthy foods that sustain your blood sugar level throughout the day.

No Smoking

Cigarettes should be avoided at all costs. Nicotine stimulates the adrenal glands, which adds to stress, but that is the least of the problems with cigarettes. As explained in Chapter 2, the effects of smoking on the voice are devastating and life threatening. In addition, the National Cancer Institute reports that smokers are absent from work fifty percent more often than nonsmokers, are fifty percent more likely to be hospitalized, and have twice as many on-the-job accidents. Smoking affects productivity, and people who make a living with their voice are foolish to abuse it by smoking.

Exercise

One thing that can help you relax is physical exercise. Adding a work-out session three times a week can greatly reduce stress and relieve the pressure of the business. This can be done at home, at a spa, or some stations like WUSA in Washington have an exercise room at the station. That is really ideal. Any exercise that increases the heart rate for at least twenty minutes and can be done three or more times a week is what is needed. It will help the body stay fit, and the endorphines released in the brain will relieve stress.

Avoid highly competitive sports like racquetball and squash because these may actually make you more stressed. Exercise does not have to be aerobic to help relieve stress. Yoga, tai chi, or simple stretches can work as well (see Figure 19). These create a sense of relaxation while moving the body. Getting a massage is another excellent way to achieve a relaxed state.

Relaxation

For most broadcasters, the most difficult time is often when they walk into the sound booth or sit down at the anchor desk. Their day to that point has needed a healthy level of stress to cope with split-second deadlines and the demands of their day—the telephone calls, interviews, writing, editing, and all the other pressures of the news business. But in order to sound conversational and relaxed when voicing, they have to eliminate that stress. They have to make a conscious transition from the daily routine of getting the news to the actual voicing of that news.

One way to break the cycle of stress is with a planned period of relaxation. Twenty minutes of deep relaxation have been shown to revitalize the body as well as two hours of sleep. What relaxation does is turn off the arousal response started by stress. It slows down the body. Just like a well-maintained computer works most effectively, a relaxed body reduces the stress on all parts of the body.

A relaxation period can be effective if it clears the mind or if it focuses the mind on something that allows the mental chatter to stop. One Zen master said the mind becomes like a glass of muddy water. What we have to do is still the mind so that the mud settles and the mind becomes clear. This type of relaxation is not some mystical Eastern technique. It simply involves sitting quietly for a few minutes and concentrating on a word, a sound, an object, or your breathing (see Chapter 1 and Coping with Stress Warm-Ups). The body will function better and the voice will sound better when you give yourself time to do conscious relaxation. This is not a luxury, it is a necessity.

Having a relaxation routine as part of your work day is effective in two important ways. First, it breaks the stress because the relaxation works to turn off the stress arousal response. Second, it provides a sense of having control over your life. Since stress is basically a feeling of not having control of your life, this is an important benefit. And it is good to remember that the busier the day is, the more important it is to relax. When it seems you have the least time to take a relaxation break is when you need it the most.

Breathing for Stress Reduction

Breathing is a key factor when working with stress. It is one of the first body functions to suffer from the effects of stress. Some of the warning signs of tension that involve the breath are frequent yawning or sighing or holding your breath and then gulping air in. It is also common to hyperventilate when stressed. This is a fast, shallow breathing that gives a feeling of breathlessness. It causes the carbon dioxide level to drop, resulting in a feeling of lightheadedness and dizziness.

As a broadcaster, learning to use the abdominal-diaphragmatic breath is one of the best ways to maintain a healthy, relaxed voice (see Chapter 1).

Stretching for Stress Reduction

Breathing combined with stretching is also an effective way to relax (see Figure 19). Stretch with care, however. One of the quickest ways to pull a muscle is by jumping up from your desk after sitting for a while and whipping your head around in neck rolls or twisting your body to stretch it. Conscious stretching is a good relaxer, but it needs to be done with care. Let the breath help coordinate any stretching. Inhale as you tense a muscle and exhale as you relax it.

Visualization for Stress Reduction

Visualization is another relaxation technique that works very well. Everyone knows how to do this. In fact, visualization is nothing more than daydreaming. But what it does to our minds and bodies is really very positive. You can look at the details of something like a shell for a few seconds and really concentrate on the shell. This short, mental vacation will relax your body and mind (see Coping with Stress Warm-Ups).

Creative visualization can also have a very positive effect on the body and on performance. This type of visualization involves closing the eyes and imagining an activity. This has been used in sports and theatre and dance for years as a way to improve performance. Studies have been done that show that imagining you are completing a task well can be as effective as actual physical practice. One study was of people making free throws in basketball. The group that practiced and the group that only imagined themselves

Figure 19
Stretching Warm-Ups for Broadcasters

A relaxed upper body improves vocal delivery by making it easier to breathe correctly and by releasing tension from the laryngeal area in the throat. Simple stretching warm-ups can help prepare the body for good vocal production prior to voicing. They are also beneficial during tracking or at breaks during anchoring to ensure a relaxed upper body. This entire warm-up will take you less than five minutes, so stretch easily and comfortably as often as possible. You will feel the difference in your body and hear the difference in your delivery.

NOTE: Do all these warm-ups in a standing position with your knees slightly flexed and your feet shoulder-width apart. Never bounce or throw your body into a stretch. If you have any pain, do not do the stretching and check with your physician.

1. Begin with your hands at your sides. Raise your hands above your head in a slow stretch. Reach up several times as if you are trying to pick apples just above your reach. Lower your arms. Repeat four times.

2. Interlace your fingers with your hands behind your head and your elbows out to your sides. Stretch up and back, drawing your shoulder blades toward each other and gently arching your back. Stretch your elbows forward as if trying to touch them together. Let them drop down toward the floor, and gently pull your head down toward your chest. Repeat gently in a flowing manner four times.

3. Pretend you are swimming using the breaststroke. Begin with your arms straight out in front of you with the backs of your hands touching. Stroke back as far as you can comfortably with both arms. Repeat four times.

Figure 19 continued

4. Pretend you are swimming using the backstroke. With the same beginning position as #2, rotate one arm back and follow your hand with your eyes. Repeat with the other arm. Begin again. Repeat four times with each arm.

5. Interlace your fingers behind you with your arms straight. Begin with your face forward and your chin level with the floor. Slowly lift your arms up behind you as far as you can go until you feel a comfortable stretch. As you lift let your head stretch upward. (Be careful not to let the head fall backward since this can injure the neck.) Hold the stretch for five seconds. Repeat four times.

6. Roll your shoulders, moving both at the same time. Begin by pulling them up toward your ears. From this position, rotate them back so that your shoulder blades are coming together. Now stretch them down. Finish by rotating them forward as if trying to make your shoulders touch in front. Continue this rotating four times. Change direction and rotate four times.

---

making free throws improved at almost the exact same rate after a twenty-day period.

Creative visualization is especially helpful for people experiencing panic attacks. One anchor was having a panic attack on the set almost every night. Her heart would race, she would start sweating, and she would feel like she was going to pass out. She began taking ten minutes before each newscast to sit quietly with her eyes closed and imagine herself doing the best job she had ever done as an anchor. She remembered a specific newscast where everything went just as she wanted and she felt completely confident and in control. Each night she would go back to that experience in her mind before going on the set. She found that this greatly reduced her panicky feeling. Her overall performance improved as well because she became more centered and focused before each broadcast.

Environmental Health and the Newsroom

Some factors related to stress are within our immediate control and some are not. One area of concern in the last few years is the health of the working environment. The World Health Organization in 1993 estimated that thirty percent of this nation's four million commercial buildings had poor indoor-air quality. The term "sick building syndrome" was coined, which is used when there are unexplained respiratory problems, excessive fatigue, headaches, and/or eye irritations experienced by ten to twenty percent of a building's occupants at a given time.

Effect of Work Environment on Broadcasters

This syndrome has special significance for the health of broadcasters. All of the associated symptoms can be potentially harmful to vocal production and add to a person's stress level. Nose and throat irritation and sinus discomfort affect resonance. They also cause changes in the mucosal lubrication of our vocal tract, which can cause vocal damage. Respiratory problems and lethargy affect vocal energy. Headaches and eye irritation make concentration difficult. While these problems might be uncomfortable conditions for a worker in another type of office, in a newsroom they are career damaging.

Little concern has been given to sick building syndrome in the broadcasting field. Broadcasters often work in conditions that are appalling when considering vocal health. One newsroom I visited was being completely remodeled while the on-air talent worked around the construction. The construction dust was so thick it was possible to write on most of the surfaces in the newsroom. The computers had been carefully draped with plastic, but the most expensive equipment in the newsroom, the vocal tracts of the on-air staff, was unprotected. The news director voiced concern that so many of his people were ill, and yet no one connected the illnesses with the construction.

Another newsroom had recently completed renovation and had a beautiful working space to show for it. What had been ignored, however, was the placement of the air vents. Both the lead anchors had desks positioned directly below air conditioning vents. Again there was no association made between their bouts of hoarseness and laryngitis and this unhealthy design.

Sources of Pollution in the Newsroom

These errors are fairly major ones, but subtle building problems exist as well. Most of us know of the hazards of radon and asbestos, but sick building syndrome involves more than this. There are literally thousands of low-level pollutants that fill the air. Indoor chemical toxins include paint, cleaning and office machine chemicals, off-gassing from new rugs and upholstery, and cigarette smoke.

One of the biggest culprits is negligent maintenance of heating and air conditioning systems. In most buildings built or re-modeled during the 1970s or '80s, there is not enough circulating outdoor air to dilute and remove contaminants from the air. Working in an environment like this for hours at a time is harmful. It is much the same effect as sitting on an airplane for eight hours and breathing stale, dry air. Pollutants and germs are allowed to recirculate, which creates an unhealthy environment.

The problem may originate outside of the immediate office area. In a large building, poor ventilation will circulate polluted air from other offices where activities such as printing or painting may be taking place. This is also a problem when smoking is allowed in certain areas of a building. Without good air ventilation, a newsroom staff may be inhaling smoke from another part of the building. One newsroom I visited was situated next to a large parking garage, and the smell of car exhaust was pervasive throughout the newsroom. This creates a very unhealthy environment for people who depend on their voices to make their living. And an unhealthy environment adds to the stress of the staff of the newsroom.

Another way indoor air pollution occurs is when build-ing managers shut down outside dampers in an attempt to save money on heating and air conditioning. Without proper circulation, newsroom air will become a mixture of thousands of pollutants that are destructive to vocal health.

Common pollutants are the tiny mineral fibers in ceiling tiles and in the insulation that lines most ventilation systems. These tiny fibers are attracted to electrostatic fields generated by equipment like computer monitors. In a room with poor air ventilation, each computer screen attracts a pool of pollutants. Working in front of a screen puts newsroom personnel in the worst possible place for clean air.

The concern of workers about indoor air quality has spawned litigation and prompted government agencies to take the matter seriously. The EPA plans to release guidelines for indoor air quality. OSHA (Occupational Safety and Health Administration) has drafted some proposed rules for indoor air quality, but it will take time for them to be adopted. Right now the standards are taken from the American Society of Heating, Refrigerating and Air-Conditioning Engineers Standards. But none of these standards takes into account the special needs of on-air broadcasters.

Improving Indoor Air Quality

Until clearer standards are adopted, the best approach for newsroom personnel is to become aware of the situation in your workplace. News directors should check the building lease if that applies. Most leases have what are called "Comfort Range Guidelines," which outline acceptable office temperatures and humidity levels as well as how much outside air per square foot should be provided.

Average office temperatures for an ideal office environment should be between seventy-three and seventy-nine degrees with thirty to sixty percent humidity. It is relatively easy to monitor the temperature and humidity using a thermometer with a hygrometer. If the building fails to meet these standards, the building manager should be contacted. It is important to check the temperature and humidity in the studio, sound booths, and the newsroom. If there is a suspicion of sick building syndrome, it is worth the investment to bring in an outside consultant to check the air quality.

If the square footage of an area is not too large, the installation of free-standing warm air ultrasonic humidifiers and air filtering devices that contain high efficiency particulate arrestors can be beneficial. These units, especially the humidifier, need to be maintained and cleaned frequently to avoid recreating an unhealthy air environment.

Improving Newsroom Hygiene

To combat indoor air pollution, broadcasters also need to consider newsroom hygiene. The voice is a delicate instrument (see Chapter 2) and viruses and bacteria can cause career-threatening illnesses. I often see newsrooms where a flu virus has circulated through the entire newsroom staff. This results in absenteeism, which affects the news product and the vocal health of the staff.

Any office has common areas where germs can be transmitted, like desks that are close together and telephones that are used by more than one person. One additional area of concern for broadcasters is the sound booth. A typical sound booth is small and poorly ventilated. It also contains a microphone that is used by many people. The windscreen on a microphone is a perfect breeding ground for viruses and bacteria.

If a persistent illness plagues most of the staff in your newsroom, look at the places where it may be being transmitted. Use an anti-bacterial spray on telephones. Wipe microphones with a similar solution and keep windscreens cleaned. Use an anti-bacterial soap in restrooms. These precautions can help maintain good vocal health in the newsroom.

Being aware of the effects of chronic stress is imperative for anyone who wants to hear an improvement in vocal delivery. An emphasis on proper diet, exercise and relaxation along with a healthy work environment should be important to all broadcasters.

Focus on Coping with Stress

A) To feel the effect of stress on your vocal mechanism, pull your shoulders up toward your ears and hold them there. Feel the tightness in your throat. Relax your shoulders and feel the difference.

B) You can recreate how the startle response feels by imagining a car backfiring next to you. You may notice that this is not such a foreign feeling. Holding your muscles this way may be your common response to stress, and one that stays with you even when there is nothing startling you. Use stretching exercises and the Relaxation Routine to keep your shoulders relaxed (see Figure 19 and Appendix D).

C) Lie on the floor and consciously release tension in your muscles beginning with your scalp and ending with your toes. You might want to tense the area first and then relax it. Become aware of how relaxation feels.

Coping with Stress Warm-Ups

1) Taking a relaxation break can be very simple. Find a comfortable, quiet place to sit where you will not be disturbed. Close your eyes and think of the word, "relax." Think "re" as you inhale and "lax" as you exhale. Be sure you are breathing in the abdominal-diaphragmatic area. Simply inhale "re" and exhale "lax." Continue doing this for at least a minute. If thoughts come into your mind, gently let them float away or say "thinking" to yourself. Try to increase this process up to five minutes or more. Doing this simple exercise several times a day can break the stress cycle.

2) To turn off the noise of the newsroom and really focus on what you are doing, try this Countdown to Center. It can be done out loud or silently.

Sit in a comfortable position with both feet on the floor. Close your eyes and begin with the number 5. Say the number slowly five times and as you say it try to see it behind your eyes. You might want to imagine writing the number or just allow it to be there. You may have only a vague sense of seeing it. Or you can imagine 5 of something. One of my clients likes to envision the statues they give for Emmy awards. That may have an added benefit! You can see 5 Emmy award statues or 5 trees or anything you want to envision. Go slowly enough that you take the time for each number or set of objects to appear. Then continue by saying 4 four times, seeing the number each time or 4 objects. Do 3 three times, 2 two times and finally 1—each time seeing the numbers or objects behind your eyes. This may be difficult at first and you may have to go very slowly, but as you do it more it will be easier.

3) Practice conscious relaxation when the telephone rings. Most of us have a hypervigilant response to a phone ringing on our desk. We grab it as quickly as possible. Next time, try stopping and inhaling when the phone rings before you pick it up. This takes less time than one ring of the phone, but it allows you to make a quick transition between what you are doing and what the phone call may be about. You become focused and ready to deal with the phone call, and you break the hypervigilant response. If you feel jumpy or edgy every day, practice stopping and taking a breath before you respond to a stimulus like a phone ringing or an intercom call. Give yourself little time-outs during the day when you take control of the event. Jumping to answer a call means the call is controlling you. You can control the call with something as simple as a breath. Remember, life is not an emergency. The news business is full of crisis situations, but the two or three seconds it takes to inhale is not going to alter a crisis. It is simply going to ensure that you are better able to deal with it.

4) Have objects on your desk that are pleasant to look at. You can use one of these objects for a short visualization exercise. You might use a shell, for instance. Looking at the details of this shell for a few seconds and concentrating your thoughts on the shell will give you a break from your work day. If you brought the shell from the seashore, you can let your mind go back and feel the sun and the warm sand beneath your feet. Hear the ocean and really escape to the beach for a few seconds. This short, mental vacation will relax your body and mind.

You can use any object that you find interesting for the exercise. Just try to pick something that doesn't relate to work—a flower, picture, or an object that has meaning for you.

5) Visualization can be very effective in reducing anticipatory stress. If you want to improve your stand-ups, imagine yourself

doing the best stand-up you have ever done. If you have problems with tension in the sound booth, visualize that performance being the best it can be. Create the scene in your mind and let your body relax. Take a deep breath and feel the sense of well-being in your body. Visualization can be a very effective way to reduce tension and improve your performance.

6) Create a checklist for yourself to help you prepare for on-air work. Keep this list on a card or in your notebook. Here is what your list might look like:

SAMPLE

Checklist for Preparing for On-Air Work

1) Take two abdominal-diaphragmatic breaths.
2) Relax my body.
3) Develop my focus:
   What is the main point of what I have to say?
   Why am I saying this?
4) Review any voice or presentation points I need to remember (e.g., place voice correctly, monitor any phonemic problems, do not gesture with head).
5) Take one abdominal-diaphragmatic breath and begin.

Questionnaire Statistics*

News directors across the country care about broadcast voice. A questionnaire for this book sent to 698 radio and television news directors confirms this interest.

One hundred thirty questionnaires (roughly 20%) were returned from 41 states (plus Puerto Rico) with the largest numbers coming from Florida, California, Michigan, New York and Texas. The top 25 markets provided 25.4% of the responses, markets 26–100 contributed 45.9%, and 28.7% came from markets 100 and above.

The responses show that voice has been a factor in hiring and firing on-air talent for 82.8% of the news directors. And a very high percentage of respondents said they supervise on-air talent who could improve their vocal delivery. Appendix B contains more of the comments made by the respondents concerning the need for vocal training.

The questionnaire (Figure 20) asked news directors to describe what they look for in a broadcast voice and how they feel about the importance of voice.

---

*Prepared by Lillian Rae Dunlap, Ph.D., Assistant Professor, University of Missouri-Columbia, Missouri School of Journalism, with the help of Tom Weir, doctoral candidate.

Figure 20

1. When evaluating on-air talent, do you consider voice to be (please check one):
   ___ **Very Important**   ___ **Important**   ___ **Not Very Important**

2. Has voice been a factor in your hiring or firing of on-air talent? (Please check one.)
   ___ **Yes** ___ **No**

3. Do you have on-air talent at your station now who you feel could improve their vocal delivery? (Please check one.)
   ___ **Yes** ___ **No**

4. What type of delivery do you like? (You may check more than one.)
   ___ **Conversational** ___ **Credible** ___ **Precise** ___ **Authoritative**
   Other: _____

5. What's the major voice or delivery problem you've encountered in your staff? (You may check more than one.)
   ___ **Nasality** ___ **Overpronounced** ___ **Nonauthoritative**
   ___ **Limited Range** ___ **Too High-Pitched** ___ **Too Low-Pitched**
   ___ **Breathy** ___ **Singsong** ___ **Thin Quality** ___ **Sloppy Articulation**
   ___ **Monotone** ___ **Regional Accent**
   Other: _____

6. What **comments** or advice concerning voice or delivery do you have for the readers of *Broadcast Voice Handbook*? (You may continue on the back.)

(Author's note: The section below was not tabulated in this study because it was not in the original questionnaire sent in 1990.)

1. Please use numerals 1–5 to rank the following factors considered when hiring on-air talent, "1" being the most important, "5" being the least important.
   ___ **Experience** ___ **Education** ___ **Physical Appearance**
   ___ **References** ___ **Voice**

2. What's the minimum level of experience you require when hiring on-air talent? (Please check one.)
   ___ **0–2 years** ___ **3–5 years** ___ **6–8 years** ___ **8+ years**

3. Do you provide professional voice coaching for on-air talent? (Please check one.)
   ___ **Yes** ___ **No**

The returns divide between the media as follows:

22 Radio News Directors
108 Television News Directors
130 Total Responses

Radio and television news directors regard voice highly when evaluating on-air talent. One hundred percent of the news directors counted voice as either **very important** or **important.** None thought voice unimportant (see Table 3). Seventy-six percent of radio news directors and 84% of television news directors also report that voice has been a factor in their hiring or firing (see Table 4). Table 5 shows that 100% of respondents could identify on-air talent at their stations who could benefit from voice training or coaching.

News directors know what they like when it comes to vocal delivery—they like it conversational and credible. Table 6

Table 3

When evaluating on-air talent, do you consider voice to be:

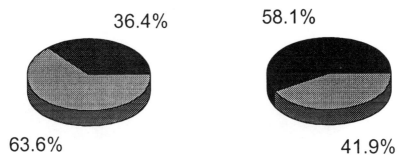

36.4%   58.1%

63.6%   41.9%

Not Very Important 0%

Radio   Television

■ Very Important ▨ Important

Table 4

Has voice been a factor in your hiring or firing of on-air talent?

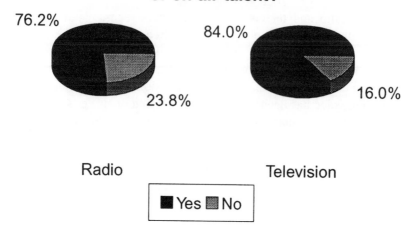

76.2%

84.0%

23.8%

16.0%

Radio

Television

Yes ▨ No

Table 5

Do you have on-air talent who could improve their vocal delivery?

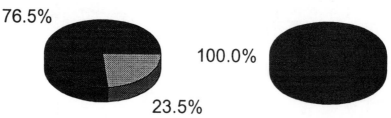

76.5%

100.0%

23.5%

Radio

Television

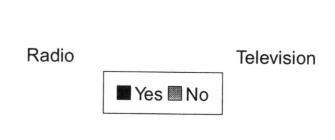

Yes ▨ No

shows the division by medium. In the radio sample, a credible sound edged out conversational delivery. The remaining types appear to be similar for radio and television.

Radio news directors also added the following categories: total flexibility; directness ("a style that speaks to me individually"); relaxed and flexible; understandable; natural; and warm. For television the comments included: delivery without a rhythm or awkward meter; warm; ability to change style within the show; "not like Ted Baxter"; energetic, enthusiastic, alive, spontaneous; engaging, unique; natural; impediment-free; and "not overdone!"

News directors show even more independence when responding to the question about voice problems. They differ most on voice qualities such as pitch. A high-pitched voice causes more problems for television than for radio. Table 7a shows that only 18.2% of radio but 32.1% of television news directors selected it as a major concern. Neither radio nor television found a low-pitched voice to be a major concern (see Table 7b).

Radio news directors report more difficulty with thin voices (see Table 8). Forty-one percent in radio marked a thin voice as a major problem compared to only 29.2% for television. Our 1990

Table 6

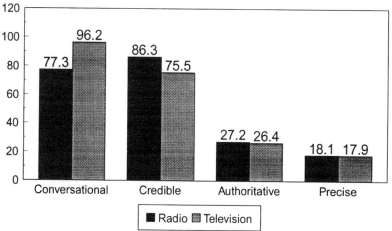

Type of delivery preferred

Table 7a

Are high-pitched voices a major concern?

18.2%

32.1%

81.8%

67.9%

Radio

Television

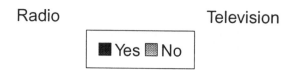

Table 7b

Are low-pitched voices a major concern?

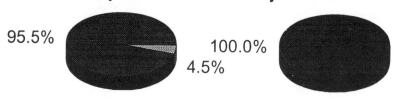

95.5%

100.0%

4.5%

Radio

Television

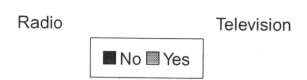

survey reported a thin voice as a major problem for television. The improved sound fidelity of television in recent years may account for the difference. Some of the difference also may be due to a tendency to equate thin and high-pitched voices.

Table 8

Percentages reporting a thin voice as a major concern

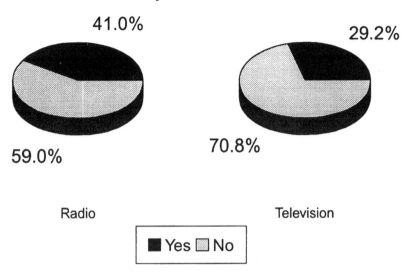

41.0%

29.2%

59.0%

70.8%

Radio

Television

■ Yes ▨ No

News directors from both radio and television favor a careful, well-modulated vocal style. They want on-air talent to perform with confidence, energy, and concern for the audience. They list a limited range as a problem for television, but more of a problem for radio (see Table 9). Failure to use a variety of pitches encourages people to sound monotone and blocks conversational delivery. People quickly turn away from dull reporting, so a limited range could be costly. Responses also show that radio news directors tolerate regional accents and an overpronounced sound more readily than their colleagues in television.

When it comes to major problems confronting on-air talent, more agreement than disagreement exists among radio and television news directors. Table 10 lists all the categories on the questionnaire and their percentages. Both radio and television news directors point to "singsong" and "sloppy articulation" as major problems. Table 11 shows the ranking of vocal problems by medium.

News directors added to the list such problems as: speaking too fast; artificially lowering the pitch of the voice; lack of

Table 9

Largest perceived differences between radio and television delivery problems

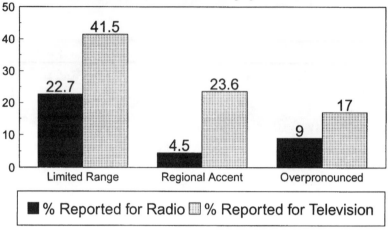

Table 10

What are the major voice problems confronting on-air talent?

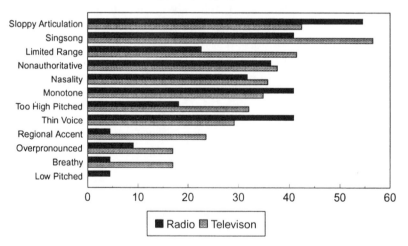

variety in tone for different stories; fake, unnatural delivery; "old-style broadcaster" voice; poor pacing; lack of familiarity with copy; reading, not "talking"; and grammar problems.

Table 11

Ranking of vocal problems by medium

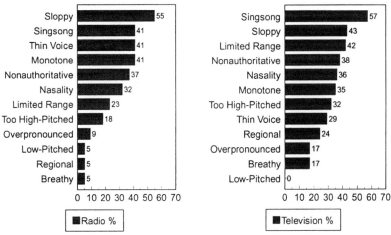

Conclusions

Responses to the questionnaire show that news directors want on-air talent to be prepared to speak conversationally and credibly about the day's events. They say that singsong and sloppy articulation dilute the effectiveness of the newscasts as does a consistent lack of energy and enthusiasm. News directors seem convinced that attention to some of the finer points of delivery will make an important difference in the product and in audience reception.

Comments from News Directors

What better way is there for an on-air broadcaster or someone who wants to go on-air to learn news directors' views on voice than to hear those views directly from the source? This section gives you that opportunity.

The last section of the questionnaires returned by 130 news directors in 1994 and 197 news directors in 1990 (when the questionnaire was sent for the first edition) asked, "What comments or advice concerning voice or delivery do you have for the readers of *Broadcast Voice Handbook*?" Following are the 63 new responses and the 124 that were given in 1990. The new comments include the news directors' names (unless the person requested that his or her name not be printed) and stations while the 1990 responses are listed by state, city, and type of media only.

I was delighted and amazed at the variety of responses and length of some of these comments. You will notice that the comments come from small and large radio and television stations from all parts of the country. This material has been very helpful in my research for this book, and you have seen these comments used as chapter headings throughout the book.

No titles are given here because all of the people who responded were either news directors or acting in that capacity (vice president for broadcasting, etc.)

ALABAMA

Don't be afraid to work to improve voice delivery. Too often, people feel their voice equals their style. I disagree. Voice can be improved and made more credible, more conversational, more articulate. It can make *the* difference in some cases of moving up in your field.

Huntsville, WAFF–TV, Gene Young

1. Think about how you would tell the story to a family member or friend. Then write your story that way. Then take out the slang. Then refine it.
2. If your delivery tends to be monotone, write notations on your script regarding the "tone" of the story.
3. Know your video and reference it. It will make your delivery more conversational.

Montgomery, WSFA–TV, Lucy Riley

I like to get a TV News candidate who has had several years of Radio News background because I feel it improves their breathing, voice quality, and delivery.

Birmingham, TV

Good voice quality is every bit as important as a broadcaster's writing style. Even the best written copy has far less impact when the delivery isn't right.

Huntsville, TV

I believe the most effective human communication is "one on one" conversation. The effective anchor must be able to deliver the message as if he or she were talking to one person. Therefore I believe that a natural style rather than affected "deep tones" is the best way to communicate in the "one on one" style.

Montgomery, TV

ARIZONA

• Good delivery/performance starts with good writing; simple direct, active sentences.
• Don't overlook the importance of pauses in an audio passage—conversation is filled with pauses, breathing space.

Tucson, KVOA-TV, Mick Jensen

ARKANSAS

Practice reading at least ten minutes a day. Read anything you want but read it aloud.

Jonesboro, KAIT–TV, Will Corporon

Diaphragmatic breathing is a must in broadcasting . . . too many people come out of school and have never heard of it!

Little Rock, TV

CALIFORNIA

Many people say that broadcasters should be relaxed and natural. That usually translates into a flat and boring delivery. Professional broadcasters have a specialized style. People entering the business need to recognize that and produce some elements of that "broadcast" style.

Fresno, KMPH–TV/KMPH–FM, Roger Gadley

I work in an entry-level market, so I normally hire talent on their first or second professional job. I think anyone who aspires to be a television news anchor or reporter should also aspire to be a good radio anchor or reporter. Voice is the only tool in radio, and the vocal skills are the same for television. A person with good vocal skills has a great jump on the competition for TV jobs.

Palen Desert, KESQ–TV, Dave C. Beards

My best advice: Take speech and voice and diction courses, drama classes, too, in college.

San Diego, KFMB–AM/FM, Cliff Albert

The major problem with younger staff is that "somebody" tells them they need to sound "authoritative" since they look "young." Well hell, they are young! By trying to sound "authoritative" they start to strain their voice and make it thin and nasal. I have to "relax" their style back to what it was when they were hired.

Bakersfield, TV

Careful! Voice "quality" is highly subjective. Personality in a voice, including non-standard pacing and "regionalisms" are becoming more desirable.

Los Angeles, Radio

Don't try to sound like the network people. Sound like people. This is the first and greatest commandment.

Sacramento, TV

I try to hire reporters and anchors who talk to people in conversational style—rather than "deliver." I have worked with a dozen people over my twenty years in news, who had great voices—but bad attitudes—or lacked the intelligence, drive, and insight to do this job properly. In all but the worst cases, I'll take brains and ability over voice any time.

San Francisco, Radio

Voice is more than pitch and articulation. It is physical and psychological. Beginning broadcasters should work with professionals who can help in these areas as well.

San Francisco, TV

I'd advise your readers not to try to use a broadcast voice (or, rather, what they think is a broadcast voice) for on-air work. Unless a reporter is very talented, that kind of delivery comes off as faked and unnatural. Much better, I think, to use the natural voice as a point of departure for on-air work, and infuse it with a slightly larger quality through inflection and word emphasis.

San Francisco, Radio

A conversational style of storytelling is our preferred method of communicating. The most common problem seems to be reporters walking into the tracking room and *reading a script* instead of telling a story about people. Often even our best writers drag down their copy by trivializing it verbally . . . or not emphasizing the right key words to give the impact the story needs and deserves. The best communicators in our newsroom are reporters with a radio background who know how to tell stories and don't underestimate the power of their voice and delivery in getting the viewer emotionally involved or excited about the story. Ninety-five percent of TV news reporting is voice-over. Competent and compelling storytellers are the people we look for, people who can not only write to video but can hold the audience with the power of their voice.

San Jose, TV

COLORADO

Use a sense of restrained urgency in your voice. Get listeners to feel you are interested in what you have to say. It makes them interested enough to pay attention.

Denver, Radio

CONNECTICUT

If someone is just getting started, such as a student, I tell them to take a speech class. I also advise (and remind) people that in Broadcast Journalism, you are writing for the ear, not the eye—so read it out loud to hear what it sounds like. Proper breathing is also important to a good delivery.

New Haven, Radio

It is more important to be understandable than to sound like "Joe anchorperson."

West Hartford, TV

DELAWARE

Don't try to make your voice something it's not. Work to improve it within its range. Be natural. The worst mistake is to put on a "radio" voice instead of a natural delivery.

Wilmington, Radio

The biggest concern is a voice which is too fast in delivery and "forced." Too many young reporters sound like they work too hard at making their voice sound authoritative. Also, the drop off at the end of a sentence which creates a singsong sound is prevalent in applicants.

Wilmington, TV

DISTRICT OF COLUMBIA

A broadcast voice should be trained, controlled and modulated to the point that you are aware not of the voice but of the information that is being delivered.

Washington, D.C., TV

Voice in a news story should not be noticed. If it is, something is wrong.

Washington, D.C., TV

It is very difficult to improve one's delivery by reading a book. It entails reading aloud to a coach who can listen and suggest improvements.

Washington, D.C., TV

In certain periods of the day people watch/listen to TV news as they do something else. A strong and pleasant authoritative voice helps to keep them focused on the station and the news being delivered.

Washington, D.C., TV

Reporters do not place enough emphasis on the voice. Often they do not realize how much impact the voice has on the communicative ability of the story.

Students do not have a good understanding of when accents are acceptable or not acceptable. Often, they express interest in trying to get rid of an accent but don't know how to go about it or don't have the necessary dedication.

The voice is the #1 detriment to good delivery. Its effect is immediate and overpowering. No amount of excellent writing or good on-air presence can compensate for a poor voice. It is the #1 detractor of good delivery.

Washington, D.C., TV

We want natural-sounding people—not people stamped into a cookie-cutter style—which means every on-air reporter must develop his/her own personal flair and style—but be himself/herself—consistently. And I respectfully suggest people listen to TV reporters with their eyes closed to appreciate the value of a strong radio presence.

Washington, D.C., Radio

FLORIDA

You must use your voice as a tool for communication, not as a club for attention. A well-modulated conversational delivery is a much better form of communication than one which plumbs the heights and depths of vocal range and emotion.

Bonita Springs, WEVU–TV, James L. Walrod

The most important factors are that talent needs to be understood and credible. The voice must be pleasant to listen to.

Ft. Myers, WINK–TV, Chris Smith

Your voice is the delivery system by which you're able to communicate to the viewer or listener. In any endeavor, a faulty distribution system can lead to failure. If you have a weak voice or otherwise poor delivery, find coaching, etc., with which to fix it. If you have a strong voice, work just as hard to maintain and strengthen it. If the viewer or listener rejects the voice, they never get to hear the message.

Jacksonville, WTLV–TV, Kevin Brennan

On-air talent too often neglect their voices. They become overly pre-occupied with how they look rather than how they look *and* sound!

St. Petersburg, WTSP–TV, Mike Cavender

It doesn't come naturally. It takes coaching and practice, practice, practice.

Tampa, WFLA–TV, Dan Bradley

Please, as an anchor, don't try to "sell" me on a story by overdoing. "Serve" me instead—make me comfortable with you. Make me want to invite you into my home.

West Palm Beach, WPEC–TV/WFLX–TV, Jay Mitchell

I look for reporters with a background in radio. They generally have a much better delivery because they have had to rely on their voice alone in telling their story to the viewer. People with just TV experience rely on the pictures and don't place enough emphasis on voice. A great delivery coupled with great pictures makes for a GREAT story.

Miami, TV

I tell beginning reporters to find a voice model . . . someone in the industry whose presentation they can learn from. Until a reporter/anchor has an idea of what they want to sound like, it's difficult for them to develop a style.

Orlando, Radio

The delivery must be clear, with no hurdles for the listener to overcome. A flawlessly delivered newscast is one of the only ways you have of making sure the listener hears what you are saying, instead of focusing on the mistakes, stumbles, accent, . . . etc.

Orlando, Radio

The notion that deep voices are better is a myth. Research clearly shows this rates very low on the list of reasons why people like announcers.

Tampa, TV

1. Good (proper) inflection.
2. Don't read too fast.
3. Learn how to let the listener know you're going from one thought to another without telling them.

West Palm Beach, Radio

GEORGIA

In a small market, lack of experience, at times a lack of confidence based on that inexperience, causes young reporters to mimic their favorite broadcast journalist. You just haven't lived until you've heard a young lady from Atlanta, Georgia, try to be the next Barbara Walters. Find yourself!

Macon, WMAZ–TV, Dodie Cantrell

Too much emphasis has been placed on "booming pipes" in radio. Radio announcers should talk like people talk.

Atlanta, Radio

If it appears it's unlikely that voice problems can be overcome—suggest another role in the broadcast news business.

Macon, TV

Don't forget to breathe! And tell the story, don't read it! Forget that you are "doing the news," and tell your story as if you were talking to one person in the listening audience . . . the days of stiff news delivery like Jim Dial on TV's "Murphy Brown" are over, be human when you deliver the news and use inflection to bring the story to life.

Savannah, Radio

The viewer decides quickly whether to accept an anchor. The appearance and vocal quality are the criteria used first to help them decide.

Savannah, TV

No viewer wants to be announced to—they wish to be part of a conversation. The on-air talent who can be an effective conversationalist reaps the highest rewards . . . money!

Savannah, TV

HAWAII

1. Better writing makes better delivery.
2. Most unused vocal tool—pacing and pauses.
3. Beware of sounding like everyone else. Do not lose your uniqueness.
4. Don't try to sound like an anchor (man) (woman). Do try to get the viewer to remember what you said.

Honolulu, KITV–TV, Walter Zimmermann

IDAHO

It's not hard to find people with good qualifications in broadcasting, even among the entry-level candidates. But their vocal quality is *often* one of the key factors I used to weed out the real contenders from the "also rans." And the frustrating thing for me in a small station is that I usually figure a person's voice and their ability to use it is pretty much a part of them that I can't fix . . . so I'll just go on to the next most qualified person who *does* have a good voice. I think most viewers would say that a person's voice (on TV) goes a long way in their opinion of the reporter or anchor. Good writing, editing and presenting can all be destroyed by the lack of a good voice and the ability to use it well.

Twin Falls, KMVT–TV, Doug Maughan

Suggestion for work on articulation . . . read Dr. Seuss books aloud . . . he wrote some real tongue-twisters!

Pocatello, TV

ILLINOIS

In a small-market station, delivery plays almost as important a part as writing, shooting, and packaging. So many audition tapes don't make it past the first minute because of poor delivery.

Quincy, KHQA–TV, Ron Heller

There is nothing magic about a good broadcast voice. Good vocal delivery is often as much the result of hard work and following the right advice as it is God-given talent.

The best vocal deliveries are not automatically the booming, resonant recitations that laymen often associate with the notion of good broadcast voices. In television, the medium is sufficiently multidimensional that people who make good use of average voices can do very well. In fact, I feel they make up the lion's share of the talent in this industry.

In my experience, proper breathing and phrasing are the main stumbling blocks to a good delivery. Part of this comes from not understanding the story, even if the reporter has written it. But some of it also comes from not knowing how to make the story and the individual understood. In other words, the reporter may understand the story but use of his/her voice is a roadblock to convincing the viewer of that.

One way I help young people to work around this problem is to get them to mark their copy on the words that need to be emphasized. Inflection goes a long way toward credibility.

Another thing I work on with them (after the fact) is to make sure that certain words, phrases and sentences are written in such a way as to allow for best use of the voice. Eliminate certain clauses and the rest of the clutter, etc.

I do not work with people on general voice quality. I do suggest to them this is a professional coach's job, and I don't want to be party to them doing something that will screw up their voices. Bad advice can get a person sued.

Champaign, TV

Ann Utterback is excellent at showing young, inexperienced reporters how to improve their delivery. I use her frequently to help train my students in using their voice properly. The response has been extremely favorable. Her techniques are easy to use and practical. Long after you have heard Ann in person or read her work you can use her techniques.

Evanston, TV

My best advice is simply to relax and tell a story. Too often I get airchecks from people who are forcing their voices beyond their natural ranges. Simplifying writing helps make a delivery more natural as well. Think about the kind of words and phrases you use. If they would not come naturally in everyday speech—don't use them.

Mokena, Radio

I think voice is a very important career development issue too many broadcasters pay too little attention to.

Far too many of today's young broadcasters never get much of a chance to develop their voice or style of delivery, because they don't get the necessary practice. They graduate from college, get a job as a TV reporter, and at the most, read about a minute's worth of copy per day in a package for the evening news. Unlike most equipment a broadcaster uses, a voice gets better the more it is used. That's why those who grew up in radio and switched to television generally have much better voices (deeper, more authoritative, more relaxed and conversational) than those who have worked only for television.

A good voice does not make a good reporter, but a bad voice can ruin a good reporter's chances for success in broadcasting. I have seen very good reporters passed up for anchor jobs because no one would want to listen to them for an entire newscast.

There is also no excuse for having a bad voice, unless one has a physical impairment that affects his or her voice. With a minimal amount of expert advice and a maximum amount of use, any voice can and will improve.

For the most part, however, you will have to practice on your own time. Make copies of the day's newscast, and read it out loud into a tape recorder. Play it back. Listen for things you don't like, and read it again. Do this for half an hour a day, five days a week, for six months, and your voice (and delivery) will improve more during that time than it would over a five-year period if you do nothing more than a general assignment TV reporter is required to do.

Here's another hint. Get about five minutes of copy together, and team up with another broadcaster who is also working on developing his/her voice. Split up the copy, and take turns reading stories. (You should be taping this.) After you have read the news, discuss it for another five minutes. Play it back and critique yourself. You will probably find you were too stiff while you were reading and too sloppy with your enunciation while you were discussing it. Your goal should be to merge the two styles, so eventually you can both read and discuss the news in an articulate, but conversational, style. This will help you immeasurably in the event you one day become a TV anchorperson who is expected to have on-air conversations with your co-anchors.

If a news director tells you your voice doesn't matter much, he/she is either a bad news director or he/she wants you to remain a general assignment reporter for the rest of your professional life.

A clear, pleasant, articulate, authoritative, and conversational voice is the quickest ticket any good broadcast reporter can have to good jobs and promotions.

Bad reporters should forget everything I've said and look for another profession.

Quincy, TV

INDIANA

Be interested in your stories and interesting in your delivery! Don't just read the story, tell it like you're talking to a friend. Exercise those vocals . . . Practice, practice, practice.

Evansville, WFIE–TV, Bob Freeman

Don't underestimate the importance of voice. Some news shows, mornings for example, tend to be passively accepted by the viewer. That is, they might be "listened to" to a large degree because the viewer is busy doing other things. I place a great amount of emphasis on voice when hiring my morning anchors. Voice also has a tremendous influence on the anchors' authority, believability, and likability.

South Bend, WSJV–TV, James Parisi

While new reporters need to work on their reporting and newswriting skills, they must not forget to work on delivery. Before I ever applied for my first radio news job, I practiced with a tape recorder. When I stopped laughing at what I heard, I went for the job.

If you haven't spent years listening to radio newscasts and watching network news on television, do that! See how the newscasters who've made it, do it. Learn from them and develop a style that is conversational.

Here's some quick advice that is not entirely my own:
1.) Write news in short, one-thought sentences.
2.) On radio, treat the mike as if it were someone's ear.
3.) On television, read as if you were speaking to one person.
4.) Don't announce. Announcer is a job title. Speak.
5.) Relax. Tension does all kinds of bad things to your voice.

Fort Wayne, TV

I wish anyone going to school to be an on-air personality would first have a voice instructor evaluate their voice and the use of it and give advice on what should be worked on in preparation for applying for a job in radio or television.

Fort Wayne, TV

Learn proper breathing (and writing that accommodates it . . . run on sentences make for bad delivery).

Delivering with authority so that the viewer believes you know what you are talking about is another problem area. I see a lot of young people here who don't quite understand this until they are worked with.

When I see a tape from an individual who has a bad voice, I ask them if this is the kind of voice and delivery they regularly hear from successful people in the business. If it's not, I tell them what to work on.

Fort Wayne, TV

Don't become pedantic and at the same time don't get "sloppy" with your words . . . be natural . . . be yourself . . . don't imitate . . . project . . . (that doesn't mean shout—one can project in a conversational tone).

Indianapolis, Radio

You only have one opportunity to get your message across to the public—if they don't understand (or get bored listening to a lack-luster delivery) there are other channels to watch.

Indianapolis, TV

IOWA

Bad delivery is the biggest reason I find not to hire an applicant. The voice communicates so much, yet there's an overemphasis on appearance. I find a lot more voice problems than appearance problems.

My advice? Learn proper enunciation, inflection, flow— then *practice*. News anchors need to develop and strengthen their vocal muscles.

Des Moines, KCCI–TV, Dave Busiek

Dealing with many entry-level reporters, I find the main thing they need to do is relax and be themselves. Often they try to overdo it, trying to project false enthusiasm or energy.

Mason City, TV

KANSAS

Many of the tips I use I read from your previous books or heard from tapes of your presentations. I would not smoke. Work in a smoke-free environment. (Our building is smoke-free.) Don't strain your voice at sporting events. (I learned the hard way too many times. I now just clap often instead of yell.) A friend of mine recently caught a chest cold that settled in his throat. He didn't treat the problem or take time off. He continued to work. The result was he sounded very hoarse for at least four weeks. I wonder if he damaged his vocal cords by doing this.

Wichita, KFDI–AM/FM, Dan Dillon

Good conversational delivery with good enunciation.

Wichita, KSNW–TV, Bob Yuna

If viewers don't understand your anchors, regardless of their news talents, they will tune you out.

Topeka, TV

I always look at reporting skills, writing technique, and ability to get along with people when I hire someone. But in radio news the most important aspect is on-air delivery. It's "the final product."

Wichita, Radio

KENTUCKY

Voice quality, or lack of same, is the responsibility of the talent.

FOR STUDENTS, vocal problems should be addressed early in their training. If a student has not reached an acceptable level of vocal performance by their senior year, they should be advised to follow a course that would put them off-camera (production, assignment, editing, videography). I'm more than a little irritated at broadcast schools that take tuition from students and then cut them loose to be disappointed by news directors.

FOR EXISTING PROFESSIONALS looking for a job change, ask for professional advice and cure the problem before you send out the resume tapes.

No news director will hire a problem. There are too many available professionals without problems.

Louisville, TV

I've found from both personal experience and from hiring talent . . . especially young people . . . have not developed their own style of delivery. The most natural (and successful) announcers often come from radio where they've had the opportunity to develop their style (experiment, change, etc.). Young broadcasters should copy successful styles from solid professionals . . . then combine them into their own personal style.

Paducah, TV

LOUISIANA

Adopt Standard American Diction. Regional identification is good only if a talent wants to remain in a specific area an entire career.

Alexandria, KALB–TV, Jack Frost

As a manager in a small market, we do not have the money for coaching. And we do hire people who have potential to develop. All too often though, new graduates refuse to seek help or work to improve. I feel a lot of voice work can be done with quality advice found in books. But you need to be disciplined and work on your own along with seeking help. I can offer some advice from my own training—but I am not qualified to go beyond simple exercises. Remember that your voice does count—but nothing improves until you put forth the effort. Also, remember to be patient and don't give up.

Monroe, KNOE–TV, John Roa

The ability to develop control of one's voice is vital to becoming a success in broadcasting. I have seen many advance far beyond their other abilities simply because they learned how to use their voice, and likewise, I have seen the opposite apply. The voice is the dominant salable commodity in broadcasting, and therefore, cannot be taken lightly.

Alexandria, TV

The key to good delivery is to make your broadcast sound like a conversation. This is a special mix. A delivery must be easy to listen to yet authoritative enough to be credible.

Baton Rouge, TV

Communication and Broadcast Journalism students should be required to take more speech classes.

New Orleans, TV

MARYLAND

Be responsive to the format or assignment. Reflect the nature of the copy you are reading.

Bethesda, Metro Networks, Ken Mellgren

While one's voice is important, it does not have to be heavy for a male or rich for a female. A lighter voice, if presented with a credible style, can overcome most voice problems.

The proper use of the voice is paramount and is probably one of the most overlooked areas in college training.

Regional accents are the least acceptable voice/speech problem in this area of the country. "Bawlamerease" is unacceptable in this market.

Baltimore, Radio

Less and less often we're seeing a deep, rich voice as a primary consideration for hiring in this industry. That doesn't mean news directors take lightly the idea of voice quality—to the contrary. We're now trying to get the most out of what would have been considered "marginal" voices only a few years ago. My major obstacle in working with younger anchors and reporters has been to get them to stop "pretending" they're something or someone they're not. When one fakes or forces authority it comes off so poorly. A viewer isn't fooled—only bothered.

Salisbury, TV

MASSACHUSETTS

The days of eliminating people from consideration for on-air jobs because they lack a big, booming voice are behind us. Excellent writing and a professional, personable delivery can overcome even minor voice problems. It's the total "package" that counts.

Boston, Radio

Proper phrasing, combined with a conversational writing style, can do more to create an authoritative, credible sound (i.e., no b-s, here's the straight story) than almost any other approach.

Boston, Radio

The vast majority of applicants have had little or no professional voice training. As a result, they lack proper breathing techniques, and never achieve the voice potential they have. Very few know how to breathe from the diaphragm.

As for advice, take all the Journalism and related courses you want . . . but . . . take the time to learn how to use your voice properly.

Boston, Radio

Talk, don't speak.

You're not Miss America giving a speech about saving the world—you're talking to people in their homes.

Springfield, TV

Words are our business. We must not only use them correctly in print, but pronounce them correctly as well. Communication is an art, if you do it properly. You have to work at it, and never take it for granted.

Springfield, TV

MICHIGAN

Voice and delivery are the two biggest problems I encounter on resume tapes. Colleges and universities pay little, if any, attention to this concern. Ninety percent of the tapes I review are rejected based on poor voice and/or delivery.

Cadillac, WWTV–TV, Steven F. Smith

Voice training is vital to broadcast communication, yet it's one of the last things many TV reporters/anchors are concerned with. Proper breathing technique, articulation and interpretation of copy can help set people apart from the pack when competing for jobs!

Kalamazoo, WWMT–TV, Mike Rindo

Personalize delivery, don't "announce."

Lansing, WLNS–TV, Michael Kent

Don't try to imitate "broadcast" voice. Write for the ear, not the eye. Pretend you are talking to someone when you are editing a package or doing a live shot.

Traverse City, WPBN/WTOM–TV, Mike Conway

MINNESOTA

I use your book regularly in my operation. Voice is critical to a news department at this level, because it is the first indicator an audience has to gauge whether a reporter knows what he or she is talking about. If the reading is non-conversational, or insincere, or if the reporter sounds young and inexperienced, the audience is immediately put on notice.

"Does this reporter know what he or she is saying?" "Why is the reporter so tentative?" "Is there a problem with facts?" If your audience is thinking this you have lost them, and the station has lost them as well.

Today's entry-level reporters cannot afford to "sound like they don't know what they are talking about." There are far too many people in the competitive job market who already sound like they do know what they are talking about.

If coaches and college professors and short courses spent as much time telling young reporters to prepare their voices as their faces there would be a lot fewer surprised applicants visiting news directors like me. I am always amazed by the sincere reaction from people proudly showing me their tape to my criticism about voice work. Invariably in the conversation they will say something like, "Well, nobody ever told me that," as if some coach or professor failed them.

I tell interns and journalism students to explore outside their normal courses for voice help. In your college theater department you will find people to help you speak conversationally. If your mass communications department has an oral interpretation course, seek it out. Some of the best news people I've worked with, from a voice and delivery standpoint, learned early that voice work is closer to theater than journalism.

I still agonize over an applicant's writing ability and news sense, but voice is right behind in my hiring priority. I tell people all the time that I can always change their looks, but I don't have the time to make significant change in their reading style.

Duluth, KBJR–TV, David Jensch

Quit reading . . . start delivering.

Minneapolis, KARE–TV, Tom Lindner

Follow the pointers on copy marking, and your delivery will be far more effective and expressive.

St. Paul, KNOW–FM/Minnesota Public Radio, Loren Omoto

Broadcast journalists should realize that voice is a tool of communication. It can affect viewers' perceptions of a story. Reporters and anchors should take a much more active approach to improving their voices. It is probably the most ignored of all broadcasting tools. It shouldn't be.

Minneapolis, TV

Be natural.
Be believable.
Know what you are reading; don't just read words, communicate the ideas, concepts, and feelings behind the words.

Minneapolis, Radio

MISSISSIPPI

Being able to project yourself without it sounding as such is very important. This requires precise breath control with the simple ability to communicate. Being able to display confidence without being pretentious, some knowledge on most subjects, hearing while listening, and the ability to convey your thoughts in an intelligent fashion and with a fluid delivery is extremely important for anyone aspiring to be the future broadcaster of tomorrow.

Jackson, TV

Speak conversationally and that means to write conversationally.

Tupelo, TV

MISSOURI

Voice is very important when reviewing tape. It is normally the first thing that eliminates a candidate. I prefer a strong conversational voice, a good storytelling voice. A good voice for delivering stories need not be authoritative—an anchor's voice needs more authority.

Columbia, KMIZ–TV, Teresa Snow

Your delivery must be natural and your body relaxed because it always gets worse when you are nervous, hurried, or reading off-the-cuff.

Jefferson City, KRCG–TV, Jeff Karnowski

Our changing industry requires us to change the way we present the news. No longer is it OK to "pronounce" the news; we have to deliver it in such a way that it doesn't sound like we're delivering at all. We must become more conversational without compromising our only true asset, credibility. Increasing competition from a variety of sources mandates that we compel our listeners and viewers to pay attention, and to certainly not change the dial. I tell our staff to imagine they're telling the news to a close, personal friend or relative. It sounds silly to some, but it's served as a sure-fire way to enhance our product. Our listeners feel as though they're hearing what they need to know from a trusted, compassionate friend!

Springfield, KTTS AM/FM, Dan Shelley

Be yourself and use your own voice and inflections. Too often, new people try to be someone else. They must be themselves, and talk as if they were telling the story to a friend. In this way, they will use the proper emphasis and stress the points they would want to make to a friend.

Use a tape recorder to capture general conversation, then analyze the delivery of others and yourself. Use this style while on microphone.

When writing stories, write for the ear and not the eye. It may read well but sound bad.

Jefferson City, TV

Broadcast schools/college Journalism programs should devote more time to teaching good broadcast delivery. Too many people seeking entry-level positions have inferior deliveries.

Voice instructors should *not* try to improve newscasters by trying to make their voices deeper. Credible, conversational deliveries are much more important than deep voices.

Springfield, Radio

The importance of voice quality cannot be overemphasized. An award-winning reporter may never get recognized if viewers can't stand to listen to more than two lines of copy!

Springfield, TV

MONTANA

It continues to amaze me that colleges and universities continue to graduate students destined for broadcast positions who have substandard communication and presentation skills.

Many schools offer courses in something called "Speech," but they seem to emphasize writing and preparing speeches, not delivering the final product.

As a small-market news director, I receive dozens of applications each year from young graduates looking for their first full-time reporting position. I am appalled by the number who won't make the cut because of some delivery problem . . . or a combination of delivery problems.

I don't care if a student graduated Cum Laude from an Ivy League school; if they have a thick regional or ethnic accent or a thin or plodding delivery, they won't be offered any on-air position here . . . or at most broadcast stations.

The regional or ethnic accent may be the most important to attack. Viewers and listeners will question the credibility of someone who obviously doesn't sound like they are from "around here." For example, I believe Boston, New York City, and heavy Texas accents just don't play well outside those limited geographic areas.

Less difficult to fix, and far more common in my experience, are people with underdeveloped voices. They tend to breathe in the wrong place, or have a monotone or singsong delivery. I also find most don't know how to use their vocal range effectively.

Sometimes these problems are worked out by the individual due to just time-in-grade. On occasion, they are lucky enough to find themselves in a position to get professional help from a talent coach or speech teacher. Some never overcome this handicap. It hurts their chances for promotion.

Members of my staff are able to get occasional coaching from talent specialists with our consultant. I also send a couple staff members to regular sessions with a professor from a local college, to help them hone their skills. It's that important . . . even in the 164th market.

Billings, TV

Beginners should do a lot of watching and listening. Pay close attention to radio and television broadcasters who are good, not to copy their particular style but to get an idea about delivery. Everyone should develop his or her own style of delivery, but individual initiative is very important, rather than waiting for a news director or voice coach to try to show you the way. This is an area that seems to be ignored, or treated too lightly at many schools.

Great Falls, TV

NEBRASKA

For young journalists in particular: You've spent tens of thousands of dollars on education, how about a bit more to improve your presentation? In a very competitive market, excellent delivery can give you the edge.

Omaha, KETV–TV, Rose Ann Shannon

Some thoughts on "voice" . . .

1. When I put an anchor's audition tape on, the first element in my evaluation of the talent is "voice." Do they "sound right." I am not as concerned about specific qualities as I am concerned about "distractions." Is there something about the voice that causes me to notice it and to be distracted from what they are saying?

For a reporter, I am not as concerned about voice as I am with an anchor, unless the voice is really a distraction. Maybe it is because a reporter is not on the air for as long or because I am also watching video. Or maybe it is because the reporters I have known who possessed what some might call "poor voices" were excellent storytellers and used television well.

2. A concern I have is the number of audition tapes from college students with serious voice problems. Print journalists are taught to type. Why aren't broadcast journalists taught to "speak" properly? The voice of a television journalist is a "tool" and the journalist should learn how to use it properly just like learning how to use a camera and how to edit.

3. I hear a lot of young anchors reading every story in a newscast the same way. I think every story has a mood and tone and the anchor's delivery should reflect that mood. I think it is something young anchors should think about, and be taught; how to develop the skill of changing moods during a newscast.

Lincoln, TV

It seems that our education system has forgotten the power of voice. We don't teach people how to use and improve their voices in school. Often by the time they get through college and their first two jobs, it is almost too late. It's great to be a good journalist but if the voice is bad the audience won't want to listen.

Omaha, TV

NEVADA

Voice is very important, but it's just one piece of the package.

Las Vegas, KLAS–TV, Emily Neilson

NEW JERSEY

Build on the basics—practice what you can through air check evaluations. Be yourself. Be relaxed. Speak with, not at, the audience. Let writing reflect your voice. Lastly, breathe!

Asbury Park, Radio

Don't ignore voice-impairing illnesses. This is one of the biggest problems I encounter with employees. They won't admit that they are stressing their voices, and often spreading disease to others in the newsroom. Take a day off and give everyone a chance to stay healthy.

I have found that most radio news people don't realize how fragile their voices can be, until they lose their voice. The recovery time is typically much longer than expected.

Toms River, Radio

NEW MEXICO

While voice quality is no longer critically important to success in broadcast journalism, effective verbal presentation is. A person who is difficult to understand or to listen to is not an effective communicator.

Albuquerque, TV

NEW YORK

My biggest difficulty in finding good people centers on speech and writing. Three out of four applications come from people who just don't cut the grade . . . and we're talking about college grads! Better yet, we're talking about people who don't seem to understand that how they sound affects more than their singular job prospects. Voice, delivery, and writing skills are critical to a news organization's credibility and marketability.

Albany, Local Cable News Inc., John W. Nelsen

Authoritative does not mean speaking in a low pitch and loud! An authoritative reporter has command of the story but still speaks conversationally.

Rochester, WROC–TV, Scott Benjamin

Even the most brilliantly written and produced news story can be ruined by a poor delivery or an untrained voice. Likewise, a skillful, expressive delivery can liven up a mediocre package and make it seem special.

Woodbury, News 12 Long Island, Patrick Dolan /

I feel broadcasters take the matter of voice for granted. New people especially must work harder and with more attention to how they present their material. We must never forget that it is our voice only that gives the listener an image, if you will! We must gain the listeners' respect and trigger their imagination!

Buffalo, Radio

Be yourself.
False, pushed delivery sounds just like that. Such qualities

destroy rapport with the audience. Voice is fine, but the biggest problem here is writing skills.

New York, Radio

It's more important to work on your writing than your voice or looks, but that said, I think a good voice is one with personality.

New York, TV

Think about what you are reading, communicate with thought and conviction.

New York, TV

1. Careful of "fast" delivery . . . items run together.
2. Keep it simple . . . use everyday language.
3. Air check yourself . . . I have been in broadcast 43 years—I still air check! And be yourself!

New York, Radio

Job applicants at my TV station need to be more concerned about using their voice as a tool. Using the dramatic pause and a wider vocal range. It is why I have always looked at applicants with some kind of experience in radio.

Plattsburgh, TV

NORTH CAROLINA

Strive to be natural and conversational in delivery. Be enthusiastic without being sensational—put energy into delivery.

Charlotte, WBTV–TV, Ron Miller

When you speak you also have to think.

Greensboro, WFMY–TV

Any regional accent will limit your marketability. Don't sound like a booming announcer—the #1 reason to hit the eject button.

Raleigh, WRAL–TV, Nancy Popkin

Tape a newscast and let a news director comment on your delivery. This should be no later than the beginning of the junior year!

Raleigh, Radio

I believe one of the most important points students aspiring to become broadcasters fail to realize is that they must become excellent readers. If you do that well, in most cases, voice training is possible. It's not always important to have what we in the profession call "deep pipes." If you can read well and express yourself to the viewer or listener, a deep voice is not the key to getting that elusive radio or TV job.

Raleigh, Radio

NORTH DAKOTA

Conversational is in. We can no longer announce the news to the people. They want to hear the news from our announcers the same way they would hear it from a relative across the dinner table.

This is all complicated, of course, by the fact that while they want us to be conversational, they also want us to come across as authoritative and professional. Talent today must be a jack-of-many-styles.

Bismark, TV

If you read your story like you think it's interesting and important, the listeners are more likely to think so, too.

Fargo, TV

1) Speak with a natural voice, unaffected delivery.
2) Breathe from the diaphragm.
3) Strengthen your voice by singing.
4) Don't fool around and misuse your voice in trying to be comical. It can be permanently damaged.

Fargo, TV

There is a very special balance that needs to be struck in your delivery between being conversational, credible, authoritative, friendly and natural.

Fargo, TV

OHIO

It's difficult for some people to understand what is meant by the term "conversational." Some think that it means raising and lowering voice pitch frequently. That produces an unwanted singsong quality, however. Others think it means sounding breathy and warm— qualities that are OK for 900-number commercials, but not that great for newscasts. A common problem for many people who don't have a conversational delivery is producing the word "the" as "thee" (e.g., Thee mayor is delivering thee report). Or the word "a" as "ay" (e.g., Ay new study says drinking ay glass of beer ay day is healthy).

Cleveland, WUAB–TV, Dan Acklen

Write as you speak. Write short sentences.

Dayton, WHIO Radio, James Barrett

I think a radio background is best for broadcasters. If it comes down to two equal candidates, I always choose the person with radio experience. I think too often young broadcasters try to force their delivery to be like the network. I always preach "conversational." Be yourself!

Steubenville, WTOV–TV, Micah Johnson

Although times have changed, "voice" is still the main ingredient in my hiring method. What good is twelve years of college if the newsperson sounds like a teenager with influenza? Some years back we radio types listened for deep, super-authoritative voices, but that has changed. Nowadays, a person with a good, solid, interesting voice can make the grade . . . but he or she had best be able to get 100 percent flexibility out of what voice they have.

Additionally, there's an element of "show biz" or "acting" that a person must develop. That can be explained as "style/believability/confidence" rolled into one.

I don't mean to suggest that a person should "fake it." I mean most of us have never met Gorbachev in person. Yet, newspeople must go on the air and sound as if they know all there is to know about Gorbachev, foreign affairs, the KGB, etc. We rarely have personal knowledge of the persons and places involved in some national, and certainly international stories. But for the listener, we must sound convincing. They need to believe we had lunch with Gorby at Burger King last week. That's the kind of credibility and authority to shoot for at least. I am not saying we ever lie to the audience. I only paint this confident style as a goal. I want a news anchor who can say "the sky is green" and be believed. The integrity must also be there to make the journalist well balanced. Great delivery with no morals or integrity makes for an egocentric jerk!

Cincinnati, Radio

Probably my best advice is to tape yourself . . . review the tape for yourself . . . and then, ask a qualified broadcast professional for his or her observations.

When someone does give you advice . . . listen closely to what they are saying . . . solicit several opinions and find out if they have a common criticism. If they do, listen to your tapes again . . . if you hear it, act on it.

I like to encourage beginners to find someone whose broadcast style they like listening to . . . and emulate it. Later on, of course, once you get the basics down . . . branch out and develop your own unique way of delivering a story, through excellent writing and creative delivery.

Cincinnati, Radio

Within a newscast, from story to story, vary the pace, but keep it quick to achieve a conversational style.

Cleveland, Radio

TV news does not require overly powerful voices. Rather, voices need to be comfortable for the listener. Authority, credibility, and trust, along with good articulation need to be combined with a conversational delivery.

Cleveland, TV

I think a good newscaster has the ability to "see" a story as they read it—that is, they are able to add the inflection, emotion, and character to their delivery, just as if they were standing in front of an event doing a play-by-play. This takes a certain degree of experience and imagination. It also requires a person to step out from behind the social barriers we erect around us. You have to let the you come through in your delivery. If all we wanted was the facts, ma'am, and nothing but the facts, we could read a paper or watch a teletype. People listen to the radio not only to be informed, but to be entertained, stimulated, and connected to a larger world. They want to hear people—not automatons conversing with them.

Columbus, Radio

OKLAHOMA

Voice quality and delivery can often be successfully altered through coaching—we use this for our on-air talent several times a year.

Oklahoma City, KWTV–TV, Tom Newberry

Good anchors know their copy and relate that knowledge to the listener by using proper inflection. It also is important to realize the job of a good anchor is not to fill every moment with the sound of his or her voice. A well-placed pause can be very effective.

Tulsa, KVOO–AM/FM, Brian Gann

OREGON

- Don't listen to yourself—as you read you'll make mistakes!
- Read for meaning.
- Talk to one person as you're reading, not to "thousands."
- Relax, relax, relax!

Portland, KXL–AM, Carolyn Myers Lindberg

Voice quality is certainly an important part of our business, but, in my opinion, even more important is reading with understanding. Too many people read words with no idea of the overall meaning of what they are reading. Viewers and listeners have only one shot at knowing what we are trying to communicate. It has to be delivered in a pleasant, straightforward manner with a pleasant, well-modulated voice. A nasal, high-pitched, unpleasant voice can be an instant turn-off and we may never get a chance to make our point.

Eugene, TV

It is important to realize how your voice and the tone in that voice affect people—not just over the air but in person, around the office, and with sources.

If you sound like you know what you're talking about, people will believe you do!

Medford, TV

Don't force the voice. It could be damaging.

Portland, TV

As audiences get older, understandable delivery will become more important. We often forget that we are in the communication business and that means effective basic oral communication.

Portland, TV

PENNSYLVANIA

Training in radio prior to television seems to provide anchors and reporters with the best prep. (Voice training is not a bad idea for off-air people, either. They must communicate effectively with on-air people, peers, public, and management).

Harrisburg, WHP–TV

Don't forget about your voice with tracking a package. It's part of the overall presentation that can be as impactive as the pictures.

Johnstown, WWCP–TV, Jeff Alan

Project. Breathe. Don't take yourself too seriously.

Harrisburg, Radio

The best advice for young people getting started is to work in radio. Radio has traditionally been the place that separates those with good voices from those with bad voices. Since fewer young people want to consider radio first, they must have a similar experience in their college work. Since job applicants outnumber the available jobs, stations will be selective about the people they hire. Those with poorer voices will be left behind.

For everyone in broadcasting, practice, practice, practice! Read out loud to your kids or to yourself. Then if things still have not greatly improved in your voice, seek professional help.

Lebanon, TV

The single recommendation I make to on-air talent is to develop an appropriate range in their voice. Different assignments require different tones of voice.

Philadelphia, TV

People should cut their tracks as if they're talking on the phone. Write and speak in more of a conversational tone.

Philadelphia, TV

SOUTH CAROLINA

I would recommend radio as a means of developing one's voice. Whether it's through a campus radio station or internship, training through radio gives people better opportunities to develop their voice and more practical experience than they can have when they're limited to cutting audio only for television packages.

Columbia, WLTX–TV, Carolyn Powell

Lack of formal voice training and the assumption that their voices are good are the two biggest problems with news people on our staff.

Not one has had a course in broadcast announcing. During the day-to-day rush, only a simple correction now and again is possible. In addition, the news people do not understand the psychology of the broadcast microphone, how to speak to one person at a time who is listening and tell him/her the story. A course in broadcast announcing is one of three during college I believe I use each week during my work.

Columbia, WRLK–TV, Tom Fowler

Do some radio—learn to think and talk at the same time— breathe—leave your "broadcast voice" at home and be natural.

Florence, WPDE–TV

One doesn't have to be blessed with a perfect voice to do well in broadcasting anymore. Reporters and anchors should simply be able to do a little "storytelling" . . . to be comfortable for viewers to watch and hear. Network anchors Brokaw and Jennings do a terrific job of "storytelling."

Charleston, TV

Few young interns are prepared to read well. Even those who had courses in this do not do well as a whole. We have had theater majors, or some with a drama background, do better than journalism grads. These drama folks, though, can't write. I consider voice preparation as essential as typing and basic newswriting. It should be learned already when someone comes into a newsroom.

Columbia, TV

I hire entry-level or second-job reporters. I've noted a tremendous weakness with delivery. Recently, I had a reporter-candidate with a Master's Degree from a major journalism school. She was willing to come to work for entry-level money and certainly had the credentials, but her delivery just wasn't good enough for me. I suggested she get a job as a radio reporter or anchor and work on her delivery every day. I gave her specific pointers, the most important of which was to listen to her tapes at home at night. Four months later, she had improved to the point that I hired her, and I'm very satisfied with her. I have another similar candidate to whom I made the same suggestion. She called recently to tell me she's accepted a radio job and is working hard on her voice and delivery. This is an important and very overlooked topic!

Florence, TV

SOUTH DAKOTA

When evaluating on-air talent I think voice is important only because it must convey a conversational style, be credible, precise and authoritative. The need for deep, resonant baritone sounds is long since past. Most broadcasters want people who sound real.

Sioux Falls, TV

TENNESSEE

No matter how poor the quality of a voice it can be improved with hard work to an acceptable quality.

Johnson City, TV

Too many television reporters are more concerned about their appearances than their voices. Certainly, appearance is important—but so is delivery.

So much can be accomplished in terms of effective communication through the use of good vocal technique. Authority, credibility and emotion are just some of the images that are conveyed through voice.

It isn't necessary to have a "big" voice . . . but it is necessary to learn how to best use the voice you have.

Nashville, TV

TEXAS

Voice and delivery can be "refined" after you get that first job, but to get that first job, you have to show you have something to develop. Vocal delivery always has and always will play a major part in broadcast news, obviously. And while content is how a good piece should be judged, the audience has to hear the story first. And if they don't like how you sound, they'll miss the news.

Abilene, KTAB–TV, Bob Bartlett

Do radio in college. Read aloud. Listen to Dr. Ann!

Beaumont, KBMT–TV, Fred Jordan

The advice I give most often is: "understand and convey." Understand the emotions inherent in the copy, and convey those emotions to the listener through your interpretation of the copy with your delivery. I also encourage reporters and anchors to sustain their energy level through the story or newscast and fight the urge to let their deliveries drop off toward the end of the copy. Since I have a background in music, I also draw a musical analogy concerning performance and execution, reminding my staff that they are, above all else, performers and that their interpretation/delivery directly affects the listeners' level of interest. And remember, we aren't "delivering the news" to the masses. We're "telling a story" to one person at a time.

Ft. Worth, WBAP–AM, Dan Potter

Reading a news story so the viewer/listener will understand it, is not as easy as it sounds. Being conversational does not mean being sloppy or regionalistic. It takes constant work and study to make the audience listen to what is said, not who is saying it. The job of a communicator is to make it sound easy to do, even though it isn't.

Abilene, TV

When they are voicing something, they should really think about what they're saying. Put themselves in the place where the story occurred. That way, they'll sound as if they really know what they're talking about, as if they're really telling someone about the story.

Austin, TV

Writing affects voice. Short sentences with a single thought are much easier to punch for emphasis.

Beaumont, TV

At the very least, get yourself a job at the campus radio station and read news on the air as much as they'll let you. Listen to the network anchors and top reporters. Don't try to copy them, but listen for what they share in common.

Corpus Christi, TV

Some surveys show that voice may be the single most important aspect of viewer preference when it comes to anchor preference.

Dallas, TV

Slow down—take your time to pause after each "thought group" of words in a sentence, so the listener can absorb and "feel" what you are saying.

Houston, Radio

Some of the best advice I've ever received in this business came from long-time KPRC News Director Ray Miller: "Write like people talk. Talk like you talk." I like to hear genuine enthusiasm and energy in a broadcaster's voice. Every word should convey "This is interesting!" to the listener. Too many people try to lower their voice pitch and end up with a loud monotone. One of the more difficult tasks I've encountered in this profession is that of instilling confidence in basic voice quality so that people can then learn to use what they have to best effect.

Houston, Radio

A voice is the most visible tool of our trade. If you do not develop the best voice possible you are trying to do the job without the proper tools. It's like trying to do surgery with a penknife.

Odessa, TV

We put anchors in a formal setting and ask them to be "natural" . . . this also means their voice and this is tough to do. What I look for and encourage is the anchor and/or reporter to be themselves. The more natural and conversational they sound, the better. So many reporters have a lot of spark, then when the lights and camera go on, they become monotone, almost flat. Strive to have them put that spark in their delivery when the lights go on . . . strive for a "talking" tone.

Wichita Falls, TV

VIRGINIA

Vocal problems on the air are like a dripping faucet. Initially you hardly notice them; but over time they can drive you (and your viewers) nuts. They can also be very difficult to fix. I consider vocal problems so important that when I'm screening tapes from applicants, I pop the tape into the machine, hit the play button, and then turn my back. I do not even check what an applicant looks like until I have listened to him or her for a while without being distracted. If I hear a voice that will evolve into Chinese water torture for our viewers, I will reject the applicant before I even look. I'd rather do that than respond to the letters of complaint that will surely come streaming in as time passes.

Charlottesville, WVIR–TV, David Cupp

Voice is probably the #1 criterion used in hiring. When news directors punch the eject button fifteen seconds into an applicant's tape, they do it because that applicant sounds like an amateur, not a professional. Yet, sadly, far too many broadcast journalism programs ignore vocal training and few other resources are available. Probably ninety percent of our daily communications are verbal throughout our lives, yet no one really teaches us the correct way to speak. We breathe the wrong way, we develop bad habits, and many of us never shake them or learn better.

It's simple. If you're going to make your living with your voice, you should learn to use your voice effectively. It is as basic as learning how to type, and for a broadcaster it is just as important.

Charlottesville, TV

Radio newscasters will, in their careers, be asked to deliver news in a variety of different styles. Anchors must be flexible.

I always like to work with people who have had musical training. Then, you can coach using terms like "accent," "staccato," "legato"—and be talking in terms you both understand.

In broadcast, either in news or in commercial production work, your voice is your instrument and your delivery must be "musical" to be both credible and understood.

Norfolk, Radio

While newspapers and television can use pictures to supplement their news coverage, in radio, voices are all we have. That's why it's particularly important for job applicants to have at least practiced their delivery on a tape recorder and listened to network newscasters for an idea of how news is presented. Newscasters should retain their individual style of delivery, while understanding communication is the main goal. Anything that interferes with effective communication on the radio will stand in the way of a successful career.

Richmond, Radio

Use a talent coach at least three to four times per year, particularly just before a rating book.

Richmond, TV

Relax and talk to viewers not at them.

Roanoke, TV

WASHINGTON

Be natural! News readers must understand the *distinction* between reading and telling a story. Many broadcasters I have worked with want to overarticulate because they think it "sounds right." Fact is it sounds unnatural and uncomfortable.

Seattle, KOMO–Radio/KVI/KPLZ, Lee Hall

Practice being natural!

Seattle, TV

Some on-air talent fail to grasp the meaning of the story they are reading and without that understanding they are unable to convey the meaning to their viewers. To be a good reader, the talent must first understand, and be knowledgeable of his copy. Knowing when to inflect your voice is also vital.

Yakima, TV

The voice isn't likely to make a reporter's career, but it could break it—or keep it from starting.

The proper use of voice is more important than any other element of a person's delivery.

Yakima, TV

WEST VIRGINIA

Develop your own natural vocal quality into a delivery that is easy to listen to. Do not force another vocal quality that's unnatural.

Bluefield, WVVA–TV, Sheri Haag

The days of the stiff, robot-like delivery seem to have left us and now the reporter who can communicate in an authoritative yet conversational manner will be the most effective. It is accepted by the viewer as if it is coming from a person rather than just a reporter.

Huntington, TV

In most cases, good voice broadcast quality can be obtained with practice. Early and constant work will help anyone willing to practice, even after a few years in broadcasting.

Oak Hill, TV

WISCONSIN

RELAX! Have TOTAL familiarity with copy—know what you're talking about—this leads to quality vocal delivery.

Eau Claire, WEAU–TV, John Hoffland

People need to practice reading more. Voice quality is important.

Green Bay, WLUK–TV, Don Shafer

Study grammar. So much of what we do is *live*. A journalist's credibility is destroyed by usage errors. In live reporting, no editor can save you. Newsrooms should develop a culture in which appropriate English usage is paramount and immediate feedback is given.

Milwaukee, WITI–TV, Jill Geisler

Seek to find training in breathing and presentation. Get a double major in speech or drama. Learn your craft in radio or live public speaking. Continue to practice, practice. Don't just read when it's time to read, record and read aloud everything. Be open to critique.

Green Bay, TV

Gone are the days of the stereotypical radio voice: the booming voice which caused us radio-types to proclaim "what pipes!" I look for an unusual voice quality, one which contributes to style!

Madison, Radio

Practice makes perfect! And breaking old habits may be made easier through exercises!

Milwaukee, TV

Pronunciation Tests and Word Lists

The broadcast copy that follows may not be the most interesting material you have read or the best broadcast writing. What is significant about these stories, however, is that each one includes all forty of the phonemes of our language.

Tape record these stories and listen to them critically. Ask others, such as your teacher, voice coach, or news director, to listen to them. You may find that you are mispronouncing certain phonemes or dropping sounds. These stories will help you analyze your pronunciations and isolate particular phonemes that cause you difficulty. Once you have found your problem phonemes, consult the practice word lists that follow.

News Copy—Phoneme Tests

#1   If you are not planning to travel
this weekend, you might want to
plan a trip to the county fair.
It begins tomorrow and continues
until the twentieth. They put up
the tents last night and will
pull them down when it ends. You
can try your hand at knocking
over bottles, running races,
popping balloons, and testing
your strength in the lifting
contest. Real animals will
provide action as usual on Friday
night as well as Sunday in the
large arena. Officials thought
boys and girls ought to be able
to attend for under a dollar. Now
that is the case. Admission is
twenty-five cents for children
and one dollar for adults. Lunch
is available at the fairgrounds.

#2   Returns are trickling in from
yesterday's primary election. The
results were delayed due to a
faulty computer in the Richmond
Center. Democrat Hinton Royal is
ranked first to overcome union
official, Jim Sheffield, for
council president. Controversial
candidate, lawyer Roy Pool, put
his position in jeopardy with
awful standings in his own
county. He was chosen by three
delegates to start ahead, but he
has yet to win. Pool needs just
nine counties to get a victory.

Practice Word Lists

If you found that certain phonemes are difficult for you to pronounce correctly, the following word lists will help you practice the phonemes in words until you hear an improvement. The lists are arranged by vowel and consonant phonemes.

Vowels

/i/ bee

plea	seen	relief
eager	creep	achieve
beet	free	week
feel	key	illegal
easel	tease	intrigue
keep	sneeze	conceive

/ɪ/ bit

trip	hit	city
pit	fit	pity
wit	mitt	pretty
lick	drip	his
grin	thin	rib
skin	wrist	visit

/e/ say

race	lame	tame
case	way	waste
ace	rage	awake
pay	state	trait
lace	date	dismay
fray	make	neigh

/ɛ/ **bet**

head	check	pest
debt	step	red
left	edit	exit
kept	men	theft
get	thread	deaf
wreck	guess	ten

/æ/ **at**

sat	pat	lamb
cap	sand	plan
gap	hack	trap
match	laugh	plant
jam	than	answer
last	mad	parrot

/ɑ/ **spa**

calm	odd	argue
car	harsh	bark
smart	shark	father
palm	cargo	heart
arbor	armor	Hawaii
parked	dark	charm

/ɔ/ **caw**

awful	lost	gnaw
clause	coffin	hall
fought	dog	sought
law	wall	auto
mall	August	thought
yawn	pawn	straw

/o/ oak

own	soak	pillow
cone	tore	explore
bone	omit	both
zone	dough	willow
clove	toe	oration
beau	hotel	cooperate

/u/ two

you	who	school
food	crude	tattoo
June	gloom	spoon
two	grew	moon
shoot	ooze	rule
blue	screw	drool

/ʊ/ put

wool	poor	roof
full	look	nook
should	shook	wood
bush	bull	crook
book	stood	brook
tour	cook	push

/ə/ above

alone	cut	money
summer	brother	jump
rug	love	circus
truck	luck	lion
run	hut	spud
done	plum	sofa

/ɚ/ **father**

amber	alter	dirt
deserve	otter	squirm
return	ponder	rehearse
worth	favor	jerk
verb	mirror	disturb
skirt	birth	confirm

Diphthongs

/ju/ **use**

union	funeral	humiliate
mute	uniform	music
pupil	puberty	numerous
view	bugle	fabulous
human	amuse	tabulate
eulogy	refusal	unify

/aɪ/ **eye**

sky	alive	strike
fire	iodine	light
time	nice	pantomime
reply	fight	China
deny	whine	biceps
bias	rhyme	bright

/aʊ/ **cow**

mouse	cloud	how
powder	ouch	devour
allowance	loud	blouse

couch	scowl	South
foul	sour	impound
anyhow	found	endow

/ɔɪ/ toy

hoist	doily	oily
annoy	avoid	exploit
loiter	Joyce	loyal
boy	voice	toil
joy	tabloid	spoil
coil	coy	choice

Consonants

/t/ to (Voiceless)

Initial	Medial	Final
tea	attend	light
tool	Utah	suit
talk	rotate	elite
tube	intend	sweet
turn	utensil	missed
town	entire	laughed

/d/ do (Voiced)

Initial	Medial	Final
den	ladder	dad
dime	handle	told
dole	underneath	yield
dollar	ending	ride
dame	condition	bird
dip	idea	gold

/p/ pop (Voiceless)

Initial	Medial	Final
pay	reaper	keep
peg	clapped	mope
poem	carpet	hoop
poke	wrapper	weep
powder	sweeping	asleep
position	typify	pipe

/b/ boy (Voiced)

Initial	Medial	Final
bay	saber	lab
bait	flabby	web
bottom	baby	probe
bike	ebony	lobe
base	habit	curb
band	obey	bib

/k/ key (Voiceless)

Initial	Medial	Final
curl	packing	risk
kitten	echo	ask
cash	kicked	caulk
keep	chicken	fork
come	wicked	slick
quit	rocky	dike

/g/ got (Voiced)

Initial	Medial	Final
gear	haggle	bug
guest	toggle	vogue

gossip	figure	plug
gift	disguise	league
gallon	tiger	drug
ghost	embargo	jog

/f/ fit (Voiceless)

Initial	Medial	Final
face	raffle	calf
fail	define	life
flour	reference	half
fun	infest	enough
fence	safer	golf
physics	coffee	chef

/v/ van (Voiced)

Initial	Medial	Final
veal	paved	love
vein	ravel	prove
vapor	avid	forgive
victory	driver	revolve
vowel	seven	dove
vice	heaven	have

/θ/ thin (Voiceless)

Initial	Medial	Final
thank	method	myth
thrill	Catholic	wrath
thick	birthday	cloth
thigh	pathos	mouth
theme	esthetic	path
thaw	nothing	faith

/ð/ them (Voiced)

Initial	Medial	Final
this	mother	teethe
though	breathing	smooth
that	feather	soothe
then	clothing	blithe
there	northern	clothe
the	heathen	bathe

/s/ say (Voiceless)

Initial	Medial	Final
such	asset	bless
steak	insert	peace
stay	essay	mouse
spill	tracing	kiss
skid	bossy	nervous
space	history	purpose

/z/ zip (Voiced)

Initial	Medial	Final
zebra	spasm	ease
zenith	music	lads
Xerox	desire	wise
zephyr	reason	rhymes
zoom	resign	symbols
zircon	used	browse

/ʃ/ she (Voiceless)

Initial	Medial	Final
shall	anxious	fresh
ship	direction	mustache
shy	fashion	wish

sugar	special	cash
chic	tissue	leash
shoe	washer	fresh

/ʒ/ casual (Voiced)

Initial	**Medial**	**Final**
/ʒ/ does not	vision	beige
occur as an	pleasure	camouflage
initial sound	occasion	garage
in English	usual	rouge
except in a	persuasion	mirage
few words	Asia	corsage
borrowed		
from French		
(e.g., genre).		

/h/ hit (Voiceless)

Initial	**Medial**	**Final**
hand	behave	/h/ does
human	perhaps	not occur
hotel	somehow	in the final
humid	inherit	position.
whose	overhaul	
heart	apprehend	

/tʃ/ chip (Voiceless)

Initial	**Medial**	**Final**
chafe	teacher	much
charge	lecture	catch
chastise	bachelor	reach
chicken	question	lunch
challenge	picture	search
chalk	fracture	coach

/dʒ/ Jim (Voiced)

Initial	Medial	Final
jaw	adjacent	age
joke	education	badge
just	collegiate	rage
genius	courageous	cage
judge	danger	college
jar	soldier	edge

/w/ was (Voiced or Voiceless)

Initial	Medial	Final
wear	question	/w/ occurs
wet	forward	only preced-
witch	quarter	ing a vowel
witness	somewhere	sound.
water	quack	
word	quit	

/j/ yet (Voiced)

Initial	Medial	Final
yes	lawyer	/j/ occurs
yellow	champion	only preced-
youth	pavilion	ing a vowel
yearling	genius	sound.
yeast	million	
year	civilian	

/r/ run (Voiced)

Initial	Medial	Final
read	error	bar
wreck	erode	ignore

wrap	moron	mare
roof	bury	tour
wrote	tarot	chair
realize	purely	appear

/l/ love (Voiced)

Initial	Medial	Final
lip	follow	zeal
letter	elope	apple
lawn	believe	pearl
late	palace	kale
lake	blind	style
lean	tilt	foil

/m/ miss (Voiced)

Initial	Medial	Final
may	remove	beam
murder	hammer	dime
mail	emblem	autumn
mock	emanate	bomb
middle	remind	custom
murky	climbing	theme

/n/ now (Voiced)

Initial	Medial	Final
not	plaintive	bean
gnaw	dawning	spoon
pneumatic	sentence	done
know	pants	brown
nation	respond	began
knife	telephoned	loosen

/ŋ/ sing (Voiced)

Initial	Medial	Final
/ŋ/ does not	length	throng
occur in	kingly	belong
the initial	wrongly	among
position.	gangster	thing
	ink	sprang
	youngster	stung

A Comparison of AP, IPA, and Dictionary Symbols

Vowels

AP	IPA	DICTIONARY SYMBOLS	KEY WORDS
(ee)	/i/	ē	b<u>ee</u>
(i)	/ɪ/	i	b<u>i</u>t
(ay)	/e/	ā	s<u>ay</u>
(e)	/ɛ/	e	b<u>e</u>t
(a)	/æ/	a or ă	<u>a</u>t
(ah)	/ɑ/	ä	sp<u>a</u>
(aw)	/ɔ/	ô or ȯ	c<u>aw</u>
(oh)	/o/	ō	<u>o</u>ak
(u)	/ʊ/	oo or u̇	p<u>u</u>t
(oo)	/u/	o͞o or ü	tw<u>o</u>
(ur)	/ɝ/	ûr or ər	fath<u>er</u>
(uh)	/ə/	ə	<u>a</u>bove
(y, eye)	/ai/	ī	<u>eye</u>
(ow)	/au/	ou or au̇	c<u>ow</u>
(oy)	/ɔi/	ȯi	t<u>oy</u>

Consonants

AP	IPA	DICTIONARY SYMBOLS	KEY WORDS
(p)	/p/	p	pop
(b)	/b/	b	boy
(t)	/t/	t	to
(d)	/d/	d	do
(k)	/k/	k	key
(g)	/g/	g	got
(f)	/f/	f	fit
(v)	/v/	v	van
(s)	/s/	s	say
(z)	/z/	z	zip
(h)	/h/	h	hit
(l)	/l/	l	love
(r)	/r/	r	run
(w)	/w/	w	was
(m)	/m/	m	miss
(n)	/n/	n	now
(θ)	/θ/	th	thin
(ð)	/ð/	th or th	them
(sh)	/ʃ/	sh	she
(zh)	/ʒ/	zh	casual
(ch)	/tʃ/	ch	chip
(j)	/dʒ/	j	Jim
(w)	/w/	hw	while
(j)	/j/	y	yet
(ŋ)	/ŋ/	ŋ or ng	sing

Reprinted courtesy of The Defense Information School.
Key words from pages 96–97 have been added.

Relaxation and Warm-Up Routines

The following relaxation routine can be done any time you feel the need to relax before on-air work. The goal is to fully relax the body with special emphasis on relaxing the throat area.

1) Stand in a relaxed manner—shoulders relaxed, knees slightly bent.

2) Take two abdominal-diaphragmatic breaths. Abdomen goes out as you inhale and comes in as you exhale. (If difficulty is encountered, complete the breath and try again until two relaxed abdominal-diaphragmatic breaths are accomplished—avoid tensing when an error is made.)

3) Neck relaxers: Very slowly drop your chin to your chest then roll your head up to your right shoulder. Roll your head back down to your chest, then roll your head up to your left shoulder. Bring your chin back down to your chest. Repeat slowly three times. (Do not roll your head back. This may cause neck injuries.)

Neck turns: Look straight ahead. Rotate the head slowly and look over each shoulder twice as if you were signalling an exaggerated "no."

4) Pull your shoulders up toward the ears. Tense and hold. Drop your shoulders and relax. Do this exercise twice.

5) Breathing exercises—Take two abdominal-diaphragmatic breaths followed by one complete breath. For complete breath, inhale/exhale to the count of:

> three—with abdominal-diaphragm muscles
> three—with chest muscles
> one—clavicular
> hold for two seconds and exhale, bringing shoulders down, chest in, and abdomen in.

Take one abdominal-diaphragmatic breath and exhale an /ɑ/ ("ah") with the mouth fully open and relaxed. Make the sound forceful and steady. Concentrate on placement of the sound behind the front teeth and control of exhalation.

6) Check for tension—if you are not relaxed, repeat the series.

Broadcast Voice
Warm-Ups

This collection of warm-ups is taken from the preceding chapters. They are arranged here so that you can select the ones that are most effective for you and make them part of your daily routine. You might want to put some of these on notecards to carry with you or post in your sound booth. Try doing warm-ups as you are driving to work and several times throughout the day.

All professional athletes and performers know that warm-ups are important. Do not be embarrassed doing these vocal warm-ups prior to your on-air work. Integrating warm-ups into your daily routine shows your professionalism.

1) With one hand on your abdominal area, take a deep inhalation, pushing your hand out. Sustain any of the following vowel sounds on exhalation:

- /ɑ/ ("ah") as in spa
- /ɔ/ ("aw") as in caw
- /u/ ("u") as in two.

Time each vowel production. Stop vocalization when the sound begins to waver or sound weak. At first, your times may be in the ten to fifteen second range. Try to build your control of exhalation by adding a few seconds each time until you can sustain a vowel for twenty to thirty seconds. Keep a record of your progress.

2) Grasp your body so that your fingers touch in the front of your abdominal area and your thumbs reach around toward your back. Take a deep inhalation that pushes your fingers apart. With that breath, vocalize any of the following lists. Make certain that you do not take in any additional small gulps of air. You should be measuring your breath support by exhaling only one inhalation. Keep a record of how far you go each time.

- Repeat the days of the week.
- Count by ones or tens.
- Repeat the months of the year.
- Say the alphabet.

3) This exercise is called the "Countdown to Calm Down." If you practice this enough, it will relieve some of the tension that precedes each taping. Establish a habit of using it in the sound booth or for stand-ups. It will break the tension of the day and get you ready to record.

Take a deep abdominal-diaphragmatic inhalation and say, "Broadcast Voice Handbook story, take one." (You would replace this title with your story slug as you make this part of your routine when you begin recording.) Now inhale deeply again, and say, "Three, two, one." Inhale a third time and begin your story. For a practice story opener you can say, "Broadcasters are finding that a few simple breathing exercises can make a difference."

(This method of beginning your taping may seem too slow or time-consuming at first. I have found with clients, however, that the four or five seconds needed for the additional breathing are well worth it. Many clients report that they do fewer takes of each piece with this method. They often are pleased with their voice in the first reading after using their countdown time to calm down.)

4) Take a deep abdominal-diaphragmatic inhalation and say, "Good evening, I'm (your name) and this is Eyewitness News." Exhale any remaining air. Inhale again and say the phrase twice. Continue building the number of times you can repeat the phrase on one inhalation maintaining an appropriate pitch and volume. Keep a record of your progress.

5) Yawning has been used for centuries as a technique to relax the throat. A good yawn relaxes the larynx and throat and brings in a good air supply. Practice yawning for relaxation. Drop the jaw and think of what a good yawn feels like. Yawning is sometimes contagious, so take the opportunity to yawn when you see others doing so. Add a sigh at the end of your yawn to feel your relaxed, open throat. After yawning, say this phrase with the same open throat, "How many hats does Henry have?" Say this several times, trying to preserve the open feeling.

Most of us tend to hold tension in our shoulders, upper back, and neck. To relieve this tension try these warm-ups. Be careful not to stretch your muscles too much.

6) Clasp your hands behind your back. Squeeze your shoulder blades together and raise your arms slightly, tilting your head back. Hold your arms up at the point you feel resistance. Release. Repeat this warm-up until your shoulders and upper back feel relaxed.

7) Place your hands on your shoulders. Rotate your shoulders by bringing your elbows together in front, moving them down, back, and up in a circular movement. Continue five times in one direction and five times in the opposite direction.

8) Neck relaxers: Very slowly drop your chin to your chest and roll your head up to your right shoulder. Roll your head back down to your chest and roll your head up to your left shoulder. Bring your chin back down to your chest. Repeat slowly three times. (Do not roll your head back. This may cause neck injuries.)

9) Neck turns: Look straight ahead. Rotate your head slowly and look over each shoulder twice as if you were signalling an exaggerated "no."

10) To relax the throat, take a deep abdominal-diaphragmatic breath and exhale an /ɑ/ ("ah") sound. Inhale again and exhale an /u/ ("ou") sound as in "you." Inhale a third time and exhale an "m" sound. Feel the resonance in the nasal cavity for the "m."

11) To gain flexibility in pitch, say "one" at your normal pitch level. Now go up one step in pitch and say "two." Go up another step in pitch and say "three." Go back down to your normal pitch with "three, two, one." Now go down in pitch one step and say "two." Go down another step and say "three." Go back up to your normal pitch. This process would look like this:

```
      three three
   two            two
one                 one one                  one
                            two          two
                      three three
```

You might want to trace the steps in pitch in the air with your finger as your voice produces them. Tape recording this warm-up work will help you hear if you are really producing the pitch changes you hope for.

12) Continue pitch work by saying the phrase:

```
                  up
"My voice is going      in pitch."
"My voice is going      in pitch."
                down
```

Repeat these two phrases until you feel comfortable with your pitch changes.

13) Use this phrase to expand your pitch range:

```
                             up."
                         up
                      up
                   up
                up
"I can make my voice go

"I can make my voice go
                         down
                             down
                                 down
                                     down
                                         down."
```

When doing this warm-up do not push your voice into an artificially high or low pitch. Going too high or low can cause vocal fatigue and possible abuse. For a falsetto, for example, the vocal folds are pulled excessively tight, and they lose their wave-like motion. As with any unnatural position of the folds, this can be harmful.

14) Sing up the musical scale by singing:

```
                  do
                ti
               la
             sol
           fa
         mi
        re
       do
```

Repeat this until you feel comfortable with these eight tones.

15) To improve placement and increase oral resonance, bend forward from the waist at a ninety degree angle. Keep your

neck straight so you are looking down at the floor. Flex your knees slightly to prevent strain on your back. (If you have a bad back, do this Warm-Up on all fours with your back straight and your face parallel to the floor.) Repeat this phrase, aiming the sound at the floor as you look down:

- Good evening, this is (your name) reporting for Eyewitness News.

Feel the sound resonating in your oral cavity before the sound falls toward the floor. Concentrate on hitting the floor with the sound. Now straighten up and repeat the phrase trying to keep the placement the same.

16) The sound /ɑ/ ("ah") opens the mouth the widest and lowers the tongue. Doctors use this to look at our throats, and you can use it to increase resonance. Say the following words, preceded by "ah" and try to maintain the wide opening:

ah	far
ah	father
ah	got
ah	factor
ah	back
ah	tackle
ah	awesome
ah	awful
ah	law
ah	go
ah	own
ah	gold

17) The word "awe" puts your lips and cheeks in a position to have the best oral resonance. This position is the reverse of a smile, which pulls the lips back and tenses the cheeks. Say the word "awe" before each number as you count from one to ten to feel the relaxed, forward position of the cheeks and lips.

- Awe—1, awe—2, awe—3, etc.

18) To increase jaw openness for better resonance, place your chin between your thumb and index finger. Repeat these words feeling the jaw drop as much as possible:

- back, back, back, back
- sack, sack, sack, sack
- bad, bad, bad, bad
- yard, yard, yard, yard
- am, am, am, am
- accent, accent, accent, accent
- sang, sang, sang, sang

19) It is important to continue to work on placement of the sound waves behind the front teeth. Decide what imagery you want to use to see the sound beginning at the diaphragm and moving up from the lungs through the vocal folds and into the pharynx. Watch the sound waves making the important ninety degree turn to enter the oral cavity and see the sound waves hitting the back of the front teeth or the cup above the alveolar ridge before leaving the mouth. You might think of a beam of light, a hose, a tube, or anything that helps you visualize this path. Now repeat these vowel sounds with your eyes closed and your concentration on the sound waves making their journey:

- /ɑ/ "ah," /ɔ/ "awe," /i/ "eee"
- ah, awe, eee
- ah, awe, eee

Next, say this sentence, concentrating on the same image:

- My voice begins at the diaphragm, is pushed from the lungs, passes through the vocal folds into the pharynx, and turns to resonate in my oral cavity.

Keep working with this phrase until you can say it with one exhalation and imagine it moving through the vocal mechanism.

20) Say these phonemes, exaggerating the mouth positions:

- /ɑ/ as in spa
- /ɔ/ as in caw
- /u/ as in two
- /i/ as in bee

Open the mouth wide for /ɑ/, round the lips for /ɔ/, pull the lips forward in a pucker for the /u/ phoneme, and smile widely for /i/. Continue to say these phonemes in an exaggerated manner, gliding from one to the next. Use this series of phonemes as a warm-up before going on air. After repeating them a dozen times or more in an exaggerated manner you should feel your mouth becoming more flexible.

21) Continuing with the exaggerated stretching found in the last Warm-Up, repeat this sentence extending the vowel phonemes:

- You see Oz.

Pucker the lips tightly for the /u/ in "you." Pull the lips back in a wide smile for the /i/ in "see," and drop the jaw and open wide for the /ɑ/ in "Oz." Repeat this sentence with these exaggerated lip positions as many times as you need to in order to warm up your articulators.

22) Repeat the following sentences as fast as you can while preserving the consonant plosive formations:

- Put a cup. Put a cup. Put a cup. Put a cup.

- Drink buttermilk. Drink buttermilk. Drink buttermilk.

Rapid repetition of these sentences will help warm up your tongue. Say these sentences rapidly before on-air work.

23) Chewing and talking at the same time has been used extensively to improve articulation because chewing loosens the jaw and tongue. To practice this, pretend you have just taken a big bite from an apple and count out loud while you chew. You can also say the months of the year, days of the week, or the alphabet for this Warm-Up. You should exaggerate your chewing while you speak.

Stumbling Blocks— Commonly Mispronounced Words

Correct pronunciation of words is a constant challenge for broadcasters. In addition to the problems of omissions, substitutions, additions, and faulty articulation discussed in Chapter 4, there are other problems that arise.

We have all enjoyed watching bloopers by newscasters. *Spoonerisms*, or reversals of sounds in two words, are often the most humorous. "Show you to your seat," becomes "Sew you to your sheet," as a spoonerism.

Another problem called *metathesis* involves the reversal of sounds in a word. Metathesis would change "nuclear" to "nucular" and "ask" to "aks."

Haplology is the omission of a repeated sound or syllable. If this is a problem for a speaker, you might hear "govner" instead of "governor" or "tweny" instead of "twenty."

The pronunciation list that follows is meant to be a beginning for what should be your personalized list of commonly mispronounced words. You might want to photocopy this list and begin a personal file of your own problem pronunciations. You should customize the list by adding words that are particularly troubling for you. These might include local names and pronunciations, as well as general words. For local pronunciations, check with your news director. Your station should have a policy for regionalisms, such as the Kansas use of a /θ/ ("th") ending in the word "drought," instead of /t/.

As you see, in the list that follows, the correct pronunciations are not given. Just like your spelling teacher in grade school may have told you, the only way to learn a word is to look it up yourself.

It is a good idea to check pronunciations in two dictionaries. This is time consuming, but once you have looked up all the words, you have a list to practice throughout your career.

If you look through the list and feel you pronounce most words correctly, be wary. Most speakers think they are saying these words correctly, but they are all commonly mispronounced. You may be omitting sounds such as the plosives in numbers like "eighty" and "ninety." Additions may sneak into words like "athlete" resulting in "athelete." Or you may be reversing sounds or mispronouncing phonemes. Developing the practice of looking words up in a dictionary is important.

Here is a list of recommended dictionaries:

The American Heritage Dictionary. 2d college ed. Boston: Houghton Mifflin Company, 1985.

Ehrlich, Eugene, and Raymond Hand, Jr. *NBC Handbook of Pronunciation.* 4th ed. New York: HarperCollins, 1991.

Kenyon, John Samuel, and Thomas Albert Knott. *A Pronouncing Dictionary of American English.* Springfield: Merriam-Webster Inc., 1953.

The Random House Dictionary of the English Language. 2d ed, unabridged. New York: Random House, 1987.

Webster's Ninth New Collegiate Dictionary. Springfield: Merriam-Webster Inc. 1985.

Two other interesting sources are:

Elster, Charles Harrington. *There is No Zoo in Zoology and Other Beastly Mispronunciations.* New York: Macmillan Publishing Company, 1988.

Urdang, Laurence, ed. *The New York Times Everyday Reader's Dictionary of Misunderstood, Misused, and Mispronounced Words.* Revised Edition. New York: New American Library, 1985.

100 Commonly Mispronounced Words

Correct Pronunciation

ABERRANT   _____

ACADEMIA   _____

ACCESSORY   _____

ACCLIMATE   _____

ACCOMPANIST   _____

ADMIRABLE   _____

AFFLUENCE   _____

ALLEGED   _____

APARTHEID   _____

APPLICABLE   _____

ARCHETYPE _____

ASBESTOS _____

ASSEMBLY _____

ASSUAGE _____

ATHLETE _____

ATMOSPHERIC _____

AUXILIARY _____

BARBITURATE _____

BEQUEATH _____

BULIMIA _____

BYZANTINE _____

CALM _____

CAPRICIOUS _____

CARIBBEAN _____

CAVEAT _____

CLIQUE _____

COMPARABLE _____

CONSORTIUM _____

CONTEMPLATIVE _____

CONTROVERSIAL _____

DAIS _____

DATA _____

DECIBEL _____

DELUGE _____

DISPARATE _____

DUTY _____

ELECTORAL _____

ENVELOPE _____

ENVOY _____

ERR _____

FACADE _____

FORMIDABLE _____

FORTE _____

FOYER _____

FUNGI _____

GALA _____

GENUINE _____

GOVERNMENT _____

GRIEVOUS _____

HARASS _____

HEINOUS   _____

HERB   _____

HOMICIDE   _____

HOSPITABLE   _____

IDEA   _____

ILLUSTRATIVE   _____

IRREPARABLE   _____

IRREVOCABLE   _____

JEWELRY   _____

JUROR   _____

LAMBASTE   _____

LENGTH (STRENGTH)   _____

LIAISON   _____

LIBRARY   _____

LONG-LIVED (SHORT-LIVED)   _____

MEASURE   _____

MEMORABILIA   _____

MISCHIEVOUS   _____

MORES   _____

NAIVETE   _____

NEGOTIATE

NUCLEAR

OFFICIAL

OFTEN

OPHTHALMOLOGIST

PALM

PENALIZE

PIANIST

POINSETTIA

PREFERABLE

PRESTIGIOUS

PRIVILEGE

PROGRAM

REALTOR

REPARTEE

SANDWICH

SCHIZOPHRENIA

SIMILAR

SPECIES

SPONTANEITY

STATUS   _____

SUCCINCT   _____

SUPPOSED   _____

THEATER   _____

TOWARD   _____

TRANSIENT   _____

VASE   _____

VEGETABLE   _____

VENEREAL   _____

ZOOLOGY   _____

Personal Pronunciation List

Difficult Word	**Correct Pronunciation**
_____	_____
_____	_____
_____	_____
_____	_____
_____	_____
_____	_____
_____	_____

Difficult Word **Correct Pronunciation**

_____ _____

_____ _____

_____ _____

_____ _____

_____ _____

_____ _____

_____ _____

_____ _____

_____ _____

_____ _____

_____ _____

_____ _____

_____ _____

_____ _____

_____ _____

_____ _____

_____ _____

_____ _____

_____ _____

Difficult Word	**Correct Pronunciation**
_____	_____
_____	_____
_____	_____
_____	_____
_____	_____
_____	_____
_____	_____
_____	_____
_____	_____
_____	_____
_____	_____
_____	_____
_____	_____
_____	_____
_____	_____
_____	_____

Difficult Word   **Correct Pronunciation**

_____   _____

_____   _____

_____   _____

_____   _____

_____   _____

Suggested Readings

Crannell, Kenneth C. *Voice and Articulation.* Belmont, California: Wadsworth Publishing Company, 1987.

Fisher, Hilda B. *Improving Voice and Articulation.* Boston: Houghton Mifflin Company, 1975.

Kirsta, Alix. *The Book of Stress Survival.* New York: Simon and Schuster, 1986.

Lessac, Arthur. *The Use and Training of the Human Voice.* New York: DBS Publications, Inc./Drama Book Specialists, 1967.

Lidell, Lucy, with Narayani and Giris Rabinovitch. *The Sivananda Companion to Yoga.* New York: Simon and Schuster, 1983.

Linklater, Kristin. *Freeing the Natural Voice.* New York: Drama Book Publishers, 1976.

Mason, John L., Ph.D. *Guide to Stress Reduction.* Berkeley: Celestial Arts, 1985.

Rodenburg, Patsy. *The Right to Speak.* London: Methuen Drama, 1992.

Index